BUTOH

DANCE OF THE DARK SOUL

Photographs
ETHAN HOFFMAN

Tatsumi Hijikata and the Origins of Butoh
MARK HOLBORN

Kiki No Buyou, Dance of Crisis
YUKIO MISHIMA

Kazedaruma
TATSUMI HIJIKATA

Afterword
HAVEN O'MORE

A
∀ SADEV
BOOK

APERTURE

ACKNOWLEDGMENTS Kazuo Ohno, Min Tanaka and Mai
Juku, Akaji Maro and Dai Rakuda Kan, Yoko Ashikawa,
Byakko-sha, Uno Man, Sankai Juku, and all the individual
dancers associated with them made this book possible. For
their cooperation, patience, and confidence in a *gaijin* photographer they had never met before I will always be grateful.

My friends and colleagues at Archive Pictures have helped in
so many ways—from looking at and arguing over the photographs and design, by handling an endless array of logistical
problems and arrangements, and most of all by providing a
base of support that enabled me to function away from home
so frequently.   ETHAN HOFFMAN

In their various ways, many friends in New York and Tokyo
encouraged this project, and this note is a small way to say
thank you: Herb and Ann Hoffman, Abigail Heyman; Jeff
Jacobson; Joan Liftin; Alice Rose George; Elizabeth Krist;
Robert Kirschenbaum and his staff at Pacific Press Service;
Yuko Mitomi; Kazue Kobata; Eikoh Hosoe; Eiko Ishioka;
Tadanori Yokoo; Akiko Motofuji; Lizzie Slater; Yukiko Mae-
kawa; Miyabi Ichikawa; Muneske Yamamoto; Mark Bussell;
Steve Vidler; Neil Gross; Fred Ritchin; Sandy Smolan; Tetsuya
and Kazuko Uehara; Shigeyoshi Araki; Hiroshi Ishikawa;
Takeshi Yuzawa; and especially Junko Hanamitsu.

                   ETHAN HOFFMAN AND MARK HOLBORN

¥ SADEV is a trade name owned by The Garden Limited.

Copyright © 1987 Aperture Foundation, Inc. The equitable owner of the copyright
is The Garden Limited. Photographs © 1987 Ethan Hoffman, except as follows: p.
12: Ryozen Torii, and p. 13: Tadao Nakatani. "Tatsumi Hijikata and the Origins of
Butoh" © 1987 Mark Holborn. Extracts from "Tradition of the Body and Dance Avant-
Garde" and "I Am an Avant-Garde Who Crawls the Earth" © Min Tanaka. Extracts
from "Admiring La Argentina" and "The Dead Begin to Run" © Kazuo Ohno. "The
distance between image and dance" © Ushio Amagatsu. "Kiki no Buyou" © 1960
Yoko Mishima. "Kazedaruma" © Akiko Motofuji. All rights reserved. Texts from
Yoko Ashikawa, Akaji Maro, Isamu Ohsuka of Byakko-Sha, from interviews with
Mark Holborn © 1987 Mark Holborn. Afterword © 1987 Haven O'More. Published
for The Garden Limited by Aperture Foundation, Inc. All rights reserved under International and Pan-American Copyright Conventions. Distributed in the United States
by Farrar, Straus and Giroux.

The quotations in this book are reprinted through the kind permission of their publishers:
p. 14: Lawrence, D.H. *Mornings in Mexico* (1927). Courtesy of the estate of Frieda
Lawrence Ravagli; pp. 22, 104: Artaud, Antonin. *The Theater and Its Double* (translation
Grove Press Inc., 1958) Published in Great Britain by John Calder (Publishers) Ltd,
London; p. 85: Terayama, Shuji, "Manifesto," *The Drama Review* (December
1985).

Library of Congress Catalog Number 85-052457. ISBN 0-89381-216-1.

Composition by David E. Seham Assoc., Inc., Metuchen, New Jersey. Printed in
Hong Kong.

Book design by Wendy Byrne. Jacket design by Charles Mikolaycak.

The staff at Aperture for *Butoh: Dance of the Dark Soul* is Michael E. Hoffman,
Executive Director; Mark Holborn, Editor; Donald Young, Managing Editor; Ina Schell,
Director of Sales and Marketing; Stevan Baron, Production Director; Barbara Sadick,
Production Manager.

Aperture Foundation, Inc. publishes a periodical, books, and portfolios of fine pho-
tography to communicate with serious photographers everywhere. A complete catalog
is available upon request. Address: 20 East 23 Street, New York, New York 10010.

UNO MAN

Dance: 21,000 Leagues

TATSUMI HIJIKATA AND THE ORIGINS OF BUTOH

By Mark Holborn

I visited the dancer Tatsumi Hijikata two years before his death. For several hours I watched him closely while he spoke. His language was one of gesture. I realized later that the meeting was a performance I was privileged to attend.

The sliding doors to his studio on a residential back street of Tokyo were opened by a dancer with a whitened mask-like face, dressed in black. Within, Hijikata wore a loose kimono, he moved with a stooped back, his long hair was tied back, and he carried a baton. Gongs and percussive instruments hung from the ceiling. His students were moving across the room very slowly with the whites of their eyes rolled up in an entranced exercise. They suddenly stopped and began to pull down screens to darken the room. Hijikata picked up a projector and began to beam images of dancers' bodies onto the walls and ceiling. The dancers wore black hoods over their heads. Their forms were abstracted, sculptural. With the projector in his arms, Hijikata moved the images into the corners, where the pictures fragmented and the bodies were distorted to greatest effect.

This display was followed by the projection of a crude but extraordinary film, shot with a hand-held camera, that was reminiscent of some early archive material of a shamanistic rite from the turn of the century. Hijikata appeared demonic in the film. He was carried onstage on a palanquin beneath a sunshade; a rabbit dangled on a pole beside him and a cockerel was suspended by its claws. In a G-string with a protruding phallus, Hijikata jerked and twitched in spasmodic rhythm. At one stage he appeared in a dress. At the climax he was suspended across the stage, entwined in ropes as if he were being torn apart or in the posture of crucifixion. While we watched the film, Hijikata played a Beatles record. The frenzied performance on screen was bizarrely juxtaposed to the sound of "Oh Darling, Please Believe Me." Such collisions of imagery, in which time, culture, and geography are realigned, are part of the tension with which Tokyo is strung.

The film was shot in 1968 during Hijikata's performance of *Revolt of the Flesh*. The event marked Hijikata's final turning away from the influences of Western modern dance. It signaled his total immersion in his native roots, his memory, and the assertion of his own form of dance that he had explored through his performances over ten years on the fringes of Tokyo culture. He was the progenitor of Butoh, and through *Revolt of the Flesh*, Hijikata's personal turning point, Butoh was established with all its wild juxtaposition. The body language and spectacle of Butoh had a form, born out of a particular Japanese experience, and had acquired through Hijikata the quality of universal theater.

Upstairs in Hijikata's studio later that evening he spoke with a poetic rhythm, eloquently avoiding any rationalization of Butoh. His voice strung together associations, chains of references from Artaud to Lorca or to the stars in Joan Miro's paintings. There was a consistent image of a silent scream, an anguished mask, linked to the image of Tokyo itself. After several hours he took a large block of ice from a bowl and smashed it on the corner of the table. When I admired the table he stubbed his cigarette into the perfect grain, upending any notion I might have harbored about the harmony of the Japanese sensibility. As I left the house in the summer night, I heard the pulse of the drums of the Bon Odori festival; lanterns flickered across the city, illuminated like a stage.

Butoh has a primordial quality. It is dark. It is generated somewhere in the lower strata of the subconscious, in the murky areas of personal prehistory. Memory is its source. Its etymology refers specifically to dance through the character *bu*. *Buyoh* is the neutral word for dance, but it has a sense of jumping or leaping, whereas *toh* implies a stomping. *Buyoh* is in the ascendant, like the vertical ascent of Vaslav Nijinsky or Isadora Duncan's leap toward the source of light. *Butoh* is a descent. Hijikata would often say, "I would never jump or leave the ground; it is on the ground that I dance."

Butoh has an additional, curious, cross-cultural connotation. In the early Meiji period there was a famous Western ballroom, the Rokumeikan dance hall in Tokyo, where politicians, diplomats, and generals might dance with their ladies in ball gowns. The balls were called *butohkai*. Later these dances, where refined Japanese assumed imported Western attitudes or postures, were known as *butoh*.

The element of stomping, the intimacy with the ground, the soil, has its roots in agricultural society. Similar patterns are found in the dances of southern India, Spain, and in the Japanese classical *Noh* theater. The seasons and the agricultural cycle form the foundations of Japanese mythology, at the center of which is the Sun Goddess, Amaterasu, from whom the Emperor is descended. Amaterasu is said to have retreated into a cave and plunged the world into darkness after her unruly brother Susano, the Storm God, allowed his piebald horses to rampage through her rice fields. In the cold and darkness of her absence, the other spirits, or *kami*, gathered outside the cave and performed wild and bawdy dances. They also placed a mirror in the branches of a tree overlooking the cave. Amaterasu, curious at the sound of the revelry, peered outside and caught her reflection in the mirror. Dazzled by her own countenance, she returned to the world, and the warmth and light were restored with the onset of spring. The stomping of Butoh has its mythical parallels in the revelry of the spirits in a darkened world.

Hijikata's dance was literally called *Ankoku Butoh*, meaning black or dark dance. The darkness referred to elements—the territory of taboo, the forbidden zones—on which light had never been cast. The dance had the subversive power of an outlawed language. This dark side also represented the underprivileged, the exploited, and the neglected, which for Hijikata signified the rural backwaters of the remote northern region of Tohoku, where he was born. Dancers have always applied movements to the body, which had been a cause for Hijikata's dissatisfaction with Western dance. He was interested in allowing movements to emerge from his body. The process involved evoking the memory, especially the memory of Tohoku.

Nijinsky, writing in his diary, described how his father threw him into water to teach him to swim. He walked under the water and suddenly saw light, which he realized was a result of walking toward the shallows. As he approached a straight wall under the water he felt great physical strength and jumped. He grabbed a cord and was saved. His leap, drawing on resources of which he had never been conscious, foreshadowed the physical form of his art.

Hijikata's childhood memory is similarly echoed in his work. He remembered the shadows of the rambling old farmhouse in the north country, where as the youngest of nine children he spent many hours in solitude. The kitchen, a dark back room, contained a huge barrel of water for use in case of fire. He would peer down at his reflection in the water, curious as to what lay beyond it. One day he picked up a sickle and slashed his reflection to penetrate the surface, and indeed he saw something beyond which may have been the essential image of his art. The sickle and the slash reappear throughout his work, and he would repeatedly use the phrase "cutting the surface of the water," which was the barrier between the external world and the other world of the imagination. It was like slashing the curtain to reveal the stage.

Tohoku, by its own tradition, is a land of demons. Akita, a remote, unenlightened, northern prefecture where Hijikata's family had a small noodle shop, also served as a gateway for foreign influences from the continent. There was even a belief in Akita that Jesus Christ once landed in the district. Hijikata's family, especially his strong, hard-working mother, tended their own rice fields. The women of the district used a straw basket, *iibitsu*, stuffed with rags to carry their children to the rice fields and then left them encased in the rags while they worked. The children's legs would be bent and immobile, with only their hands free to play with their faces and wipe their tears. The crouched posture and the bent legs of the country people passed into Hijikata's dance vocabulary. His pupil, Yoko Ashikawa, would adopt the posture after her finale, and instead of bowing she would stick out her tongue like an ugly child.

Growing up in the 1930s as the youngest of nine children in a small northern farming village would have been severe, like the climate. Hijikata's father loved *Gidayu*,[1] a form of dramatic balladry, and he drank all day. The child in his neglected solitude lived with the phantoms of the north who lurked in the farmhouse. There was the *warashi*, a child phantom which was believed to lie somewhere in every room. There was also the *kazedaruma*, the

wind spirit, who would come with the blizzards, open the door, and let himself in to warm himself by the fire, where he would melt. "I wore the wind for my kimono,"[2] said Hijikata, speaking of his childhood. The elemental forces of winds and cold became the substances of his dance.

In 1972, Hijikata introduced the curious posture of the bent knees, using three outstanding women dancers, Yoko Ashikawa, Momoko Nishina, and Saga Kobayashi. They danced to *Gidayu* music wearing wooden clogs. Walking with bandy legs like the Japanese farmer then became one of Hijikata's basic positions. The dancer would stand on the outer sides of the feet, balanced with extreme tension, trembling slightly. The dancer's body was then open to accept the wind, and in that open posture the dancer could be transformed into any elemental form.

The Tohoku association was used more explicitly by Hijikata not long before his death in January 1986. He organized a number of performances in Tokyo of what he called *Tohokukabuki*, a risky and contradictory combination of the wild country and the traditional popular theater of Edo, with which he was attempting to popularize Butoh. He told an English theater director, "I come from Tohoku, but there is Tohoku in everybody. There is even Tohoku in England." Tohoku had ceased to be a geographical location; it had become a territory of the imagination. When asked about the philosophy behind Butoh, Hijikata once said, "There is no philosophy before Butoh. It is only possible that a philosophy may come out of Butoh." The origins of Butoh reside in a wild land inhabited by elemental spirits, which the rational mind cannot reach.

Butoh, like many other Japanese concepts, is defined by its very evasion of definition. It is a wide word. It is both theater and dance, yet it has no choreographical conventions. It is a subversive force, through which conventions are overturned. As such, it must exist somewhere on the social periphery. It is a popular spectacle, unlike the classical theater of *Noh* with its elaborate vocabulary of gesture, yet it is esoteric. It is a force of liberation, especially within the conformist Japanese social structure, yet it is born out of extreme discipline. In the midst of a culture of exceptional visual harmony, it employs a vocabulary of ugliness. Butoh transcends its Japanese location, but only in Japan of the postwar period could such a force take form. Its imagery may be archetypal, but the exploration of memory and primary roots is born out of contemporary culture. It is both a response and a contradiction to Tokyo itself, a city that grows in contradictory fashion back into its own past, into its sense of Edo identity, as rapidly as it advances into the synthetic to become the electronic breeder of the future.

The growth of Butoh involved a search for a form true to the Japanese experience. Inevitably it entailed the rejection of elements of imitative culture, the results of the Japanese assimilation of Western style. Yet at the extreme point at which it took root, on the outer edge of Japanese culture, Butoh found common ground with shaman and seer. Antonin Artaud had realized—through the spectacle of Balinese dance at the colonial exhibition in Paris in 1931—the possibility of overturning the notions of the Western stage, dependent as he described it on the "stuttering" of dialogue. The alien quality of the Balinese dance, which implied a language to which he had not the key, only excited him further.

Artaud, whose collected writing has been translated into Japanese, would indeed have found fulfillment of a vision through Butoh, which in true Japanese assimilative fashion took on the Artaudian theory of theater as spectacle, as it did the native Japanese myth. The Japanese culture from which Butoh emerges is both insular and fervently non-Western, yet also finds its parallel in its cultural antithesis, in Spain, with all its African influences. The spirit of Butoh may be close to the Spanish spirit of *duende*, lyrically defined by Federico García Lorca, just as flamenco or the architecture of Gaudí have found translation into modern Japanese sensibility.

Butoh found its first public, beyond the inner world of the informed Japanese, outside Japan. Dance groups, asserting their original inspiration from Hijikata, found enthusiastic public response in Europe and America, where Western audiences engaged in spectacles only witnessed in Japan by the Japanese cultural underground. The change of context, like all translation, may have distorted the original meaning. It confirmed the accessibility of Butoh as spectacle, even if the translation dampened the subversive fire. What is visually pleasing on a Western stage in this decade has little relation to the fuse that Hijikata lit in front of a small Tokyo audience more than twenty years ago. The phenomenon of Butoh has changed from its origins in the dance of Hijikata to encompass a diverse range of performance, even to transcend its Japanese origins and take form on other continents.

Western dance had been introduced to Japan at the turn of the century, not in the spirit of enthusiasm, but in the mood of modernization that characterized Japan's industrialization and transformation. As with many such cultural transpositions, the Japanese had no discipline or foundation for approaching ballet, though its popularity flourished like the Rokumeikan dance hall in an era of change. The results, however, were superficial. The discipline of Western classical dance and its demands on the body were totally alien. The history of seventy or more years of Western dance in Japan has been described by one Japanese commentator as "merely a long series of errors."[3]

No tradition of Western modern dance has been established in Japan, although *Die Neue Tanz* made a great impression before World War II. It developed through individual teachers such as Takaya Eguchi, a pupil of Mary Wigman. Eguchi had been instrumental in introducing the German modern dance to Japan. In the late 1940s, soon after the war ended, Hijikata arrived in Tokyo from the far north with a bag of rice, a precious gift at the time, as an offering for Eguchi in the hope of being taken in to become his pupil. Unfortunately for Hijikata, Eguchi was working closely with Kazuo Ohno, who had been his pupil before the war, so Hijikata handed over the rice and returned home to the north.

The work of Ohno, who was more than twenty years older than Hijikata and is still dancing with renewed energy, forms the most remarkable bridge between the introduction of modern dance from the West and the birth of an original dance from within Japan. Beginning in 1954, Ohno collaborated with Hijikata many times. Ohno, one of the generative forces of Butoh, strides across Eastern and Western tradition in an extraordinary career both within and outside Japan. In 1934 he was profoundly influenced by seeing Harold Kreuzberg dance. But the real stimulus to his life's work occurred in 1928 when he saw the Spanish ballet dancer Antonia Mercé, known as La Argentina, at the Imperial Theater in Tokyo. Ohno said, "The dance of La Argentina invited people to a sea of excitement. She embodied dance, literature, music, and art, and furthermore she represented love and pain in real life. She would have said, 'It was not my art that moved people. I simply received all things that moved me as they were, and I try to pass them to you. I am simply a servant conveying these things to you.' " Lorca wrote an homage to La Argentina in which he described the dancer's lines of movement, the zigzags and rapid curves, with a sense of perfume and geometry. She formed the bridge between the classical ballet and her native flamenco and folk dance.

Ohno harbored his admiration for La Argentina for nearly fifty years, until 1977, when he first performed his own homage in a solo dance lasting ninety minutes. *Admiring La Argentina* as performed by Ohno today, in his eighties, in full makeup and flowing dress, is a great piece of transformative theater. In his finale he takes on the sensual persona of the young woman with passion, to the sound of Maria Callas singing *In quelle trine morbide* from *Manon Lescaut*. There is also the sound of La Argentina's castanets. Butoh, through Ohno, crossed cultural frontiers, inspired again by the power of memory.

The route to such moments as Hijikata's *Revolt of the Flesh* or Ohno's *Admiring La Argentina* starts in the aftermath of the year 1945. Ohno had been captured by the Australian forces in New Guinea and returned to Japan in 1946. He immediately resumed study with Eguchi. He danced regularly in Kanda and performed publicly with the dancer Mitsuko Ando. In 1952 he saw Marcel Carné's film *Les Enfants du Paradis*. He repeatedly returned to the film, fascinated by Jean-Louis Barrault's performance. Barrault's role (with whitened face and the innocence of a Pierrot) provided Ohno with another element for his own style. The mood of *Les Enfants du Paradis* and Jacques Prévert's script with the convention of theater within theater—in which the screen opened onto the curtains of a stage, which then drew back to open the play within the film—provided the perfect image of a Japanese theatrical sensibility. The lyrical rise to fame from humble origins on the street of crime was also an appropriate fantasy image for a depressed and defeated nation.

Hijikata came to Tokyo in the 1950s and studied a number of different dance styles, including flamenco. He worked with Mitsuko Ando, who was greatly influenced by jazz and American modern dance. Hijikata lived in poverty in an apartment house with several artists, including On Kawara. In 1957 he saw Kurosawa's film *Yoidore Tenshi (The Drunken Angel)*. He identified with the Toshiro Mifune character and he closely watched the film's depiction of the dance halls of Tokyo under the American occupation. Hijikata saved money from working in a laundry to buy a white suit and go to such a dance hall, where Japanese girls catered mostly to American officers. He had taken on the Mifune role. The humiliation of defeat had meant a total loss of identity.

Out of that void came the need for a form with which to constitute his own art. The strands of *Die Neue Tanz*, American modern dance, and flamenco were all technical foundations from which a truly Japanese dance could emerge if the memory could be evoked with sufficient accuracy, and if the disparate strands of influence could be synthesized. The assimilation of alien elements, from Chinese or Western culture, to create a hybrid form that was still essentially Japanese, was a repeated pattern. Synthesis had been a Japanese cultural strategy for centuries.

Hijikata's debut as choreographer and dancer was scandalous. He had approached Yukio Mishima for permission to adapt the homosexual theme of his novel *Kinjiki (Forbidden Colors*, 1951) for the stage. The performance was held in May 1959 at an event for new dancers organized by the official body, the All Japan Artistic Dance Association, now known as the Modern Dance Association. The short dance was performed without music. Ohno's son, Yoshito, who was still a young boy, enacted sex with a chicken squeezed between his thighs and then succumbed to the advances of Hijikata. The audience was outraged and Mishima was greatly impressed. Hijikata was subsequently banned by the Modern Dance Association, outlawed as a dangerous dancer. After seeing the performance, the photographer Eikoh Hosoe went backstage and introduced himself to Hijikata. Hosoe was fascinated by modern dance and he now found in Hijikata the perfect model. Hosoe's photographs of Hijikata and other dancers, including Kazuo and Yoshito Ohno, were exhibited the next year in Tokyo. In the introduction to the catalog Mishima wrote, "I received secret information that Mr. Tatsumi Hijikata is to perform a heretical ceremony again. I look forward to it and must be prepared with black masks and mysterious perfumes for the night. The classics and the avant-garde have come to a crisis."

Mishima found in Hijikata an artist who was a man of the body in contrast to his own cerebral brilliance and frustrating physical imbalance. Hijikata had a rustic directness of nature in contrast to Mishima's refinement. Hijikata's debut had shockingly probed the areas of taboo that fascinated the novelist. Mishima had struggled to create a language with which he could describe the sensuality of the male body, inspired, he declared, by Guido Reni's painting of Saint Sebastian. Hijikata had the facility to transmit that sensuality with a purely physical language while Mishima could only grapple with the inadequacy of the written word. Hijikata closed for Mishima the cleavage between the word and action which so obsessed him. In turn Mishima provided Hijikata with the erudition and imagination of a great writer in full creative flow. Between them, the gulf that separated the man of the body and the man of the mind was closed. Butoh was clearly an art of the body and the mind.

Hosoe was invited to photograph Mishima in 1961 for the frontispiece of a forthcoming book of the writer's essays. Hosoe was chosen because Mishima wanted to be photographed like Hijikata. This assignment led to an extended collaboration between Hosoe and Mishima that was published in 1963 as *Barakei (Killed by Roses)* and again shortly after the writer's death as *Ordeal by Roses* in 1971. Hijikata and his wife, the dancer Akiko Motofuji, are the other models in the celebrated book, much of which was shot in Hijikata's studio. Mishima enjoyed his visits to the dancer's studio, where he would frequently dress up and dance himself. He could extend his own sense of performance in the company of Hijikata. Mishima contributed to Hijikata's dance a banner with his calligraphy, in which the title *Hangi Dai-tokan* was inscribed. The meaning of the title, which refers to an unprecedented dance created through the sacrifice of the body, had particular reference to Mishima's own course. Hijikata would later display the banner above his performances in tribute to his friend.

The literary connections were especially important in Hijikata's early work. He was strongly attracted to Lautréamont, Jean Genet, and the Marquis de Sade. In the 1960s, a decade of extreme rebellion as in the West, the literature of revolt gained currency in Japan. Hijikata's close friend Tatsuhiko Shibusawa translated De Sade's *One Hundred Days of Sodom* into Japanese. Taboo and forbidden eroticism were important areas in Hijikata's exploration. In 1960, Hijikata persuaded Ohno to dance the role of the old male prostitute, Divine, in Genet's *Notre Dame des Fleurs*, a performance they took to the streets and which was photographed by William Klein. Hijikata in black hood and Kazuo Ohno garlanded in flowers, together with Yoshito Ohno, appear at the beginning of Klein's book *Tokyo* (1961).

Japanese Dadaists, who were pioneering Performance Art in Tokyo in the 1960s, greatly admired Hijikata's theatrical techniques. They regarded his overthrow of Japanese dance conventions as in the true spirit of Dada revolt. Hijikata's famous performances of the period included *The Blind Masseur* (1963), in which he took the role of a traditional masseur in white on a stage covered with tatami mats, to the accompaniment of women playing *samisen*. In *Rose Dance* (1965) he employed the principles of Chinese medicine, decorating the stage with diagrams and body charts. The skin on his back was painted as if the surface had been peeled aside to reveal the organs beneath. He was precisely investigating the layers of the body and his own physical structure even as he descended into the depths of the subconscious.

The metaphorical stripping back of the flesh has its parallel in Mishima's own conflict between the spirit and the flesh that he described in his essay *Sun and Steel* (1970). Mishima wrote of breaking down the division between flesh and spirit, and of establishing a link between ideas and the body in the belief that the body and mind can both create their own miniature universe. This exploration by Hijikata corresponded to Mishima's own physical transformation—the exaggeration of his physique in the gym. Both took place within a culture that, unlike Western classical tradition, had no history of the body at the center of either aesthetic or philosophic preoccupation.

The revolt, to which Hijikata as the architect of *Ankoku Butoh* was party, pervaded all areas of Japanese art in the 1960s. Butoh emerged alongside such films as Nagisa Oshima's *Diary of a Shinjuku Thief* (1968), a fragmented journey through the Tokyo subculture, or beside the performances of the theater group *Tenjosajiki*, founded by the poet Shuji Terayama. *Tenjosajiki*, defined as a laboratory of play, had the quality of a surreal and anarchic circus. One of the founders of *Tenjosajiki*, the graphic designer Tadanori Yokoo, remembers hanging posters for the theater group across the center of Tokyo, from Shibuya to Aoyama. When he returned the next day all the posters had been removed by admirers. The real drama of the theater had begun with Yokoo's act of hanging the posters. The city was in a mood of smoldering creative action.

In that fertile period no area of life was immune from the political movement. The New Left emerged among Japanese students in 1965 and its activities reached a climax two or three years later. Hijikata may have sympathized with the New Left, but there was no conscious collaboration. The New Left could be distinguished from the old wing of the Communist Party by its appreciation for a cultural revolution. It supported cultural figures who were not necessarily mouthpieces of the Communist Party.

The riots at the Democratic National Convention in Chicago and in the streets of Paris in 1968 were matched in Tokyo by the spectacle of revolt on an unprecedented scale. Images of these events were distributed universally and created a sense of historical theater exercised through physical force. The body itself was the ammunition for revolt, as phalanxes of helmeted youths took to the streets or awaited police charges at the barricades. In Paris in May 1968, when the students occupied the Théâtre de l'Odéon, they found a portrait of Artaud in Jean-Louis Barrault's office. "He has stolen Artaud!" they declared.[4] Artaud, the dissident, had challenged a theater dependent on language with a theater of the body. Theatrical revolt was merged with the public theater of rebellion that exploded in every capital of the Western world, as it did in Tokyo. The body was the language.

Ryozen Torii, *Tatsumi Hijikata*, Revolt of the Flesh

In 1968 Hijikata was outside the public eye in preparation for *Revolt of the Flesh*. In the previous year he had returned to Tohoku with Eikoh Hosoe to produce the dance drama *Kamaitachi*. They were both rediscovering their personal roots. The narrative of the drama was symbolic with reference to the nuclear age. It was based on Hosoe's childhood memory of the late war years. They had collaborated in 1960 on a short symbolic film, *Navel and Atomic Bomb*, in which Hijikata had taken on another demonic role, emerging from the sea to steal the navel of a child. In *Kamaitachi* they improvised the dance sequence in the fields among the villagers of the north. Hijikata's role was that of the innocent, the fool, possessed by the spirit of a demon, who haunted the rice fields. Tadanori Yokoo designed the poster for the exhibition and publication of *Kamaitachi* (1968). Hijikata stamped each silk-screened image with the prints of his hands dipped in gold ink. Every stage of the production of the exhibition and publication was a form of ritualized theater.

For almost a year before performing *Revolt of the Flesh*, Hijikata withdrew into a period of introspection. In the preceding month he brought his body to peak condition. He ran every day and fasted on a diet of milk and miso soup. He gave his body a deep tan with artificial lights. He was thirty-nine years old. Watching his performance, which lasted two hours, Yoko Ashikawa, his leading pupil, noticed how he became younger as the performance progressed. Hijikata's revolt involved attaining a body in perfect balance. In contradiction to the physical decline of aging, he moved back in time; he appeared as a man of thirty-five, then twenty-nine, eighteen, then twelve years old. This, thought Ashikawa, was the secret of dance.

Tadao Nakatani, *Tatsumi Hijikata*, Revolt of the Flesh

Tadao Nakatani, *Tatsumi Hijikata*, Revolt of the Flesh

Revolt of the Flesh had a subtitle, *Tatsumi Hijikata and the Japanese*, which both asserted a national identity and separated Hijikata from his national origins. The performance contained movements reminiscent of Western dance, but it was the last time he would employ such forms. *Revolt of the Flesh* was a turning point for Hijikata, as it was for Butoh. A phase of his life was completed. After 1970, the year of Mishima's suicide, he felt a sense of liberation. He was entering unexplored territory. He was determined to reacquire the innocence of a child by not thinking too much. He wanted to reconstruct what he saw as the child's wisdom, through his own past. "Now I am a frog, far away from the shadow of an idea," he once wrote.

His withdrawal into a new creative period involved close work with Yoko Ashikawa. He claimed he was "the image" and she "the dictionary." They went to university campuses and performed among the students, then withdrew again into intense and isolated development. The dancers who had been influenced by Hijikata found their independence in this period. The first wave of Butoh, which had emerged from Hijikata and Ohno, was over. Another important dancer, Akira Kasai, who had worked with Hijikata's *Ankoku Butoh*, left Japan to study the Rudolf Steiner movement in Germany. Butoh was splitting into multiple forms.

In 1972, Akaji Maro, a former actor with the *Jokyo Gekijo* theater who had lived with Hijikata for nearly three years, formed his own group, *Dai Rakuda Kan* (The Great Camel Battleship). The camel was chosen as a creature that had walked the Silk Route, the traditional line of communication between East and West, connecting Con-

stantinople and China. Maro enlarged the spectacle of Butoh and chose a symbol that bridged the East-West divide. In 1975, Ushio Amagatsu, a former member of *Dai Rakuda Kan*, established *Sankai Juku*, a group that has taken Butoh out of Japan. Perhaps more than any other dancers, they have brought Butoh to a wide international public. Amagatsu's imagery involves a return to the primordial being.

In 1978, *Kinkan Shonen (The Kumquat Seed)* was premiered in Tokyo. Amagatsu gave the piece the subtitle, *A Young Boy's Dream of the Origins of Life and Death*. It referred to Amagatsu's own life on the coast of Japan and involved a creation myth and the ocean. Amagatsu stated that a figure hanging head down at the end of *Kinkan Shonen* recalled the moment of birth. In *Jomon Sho*, which *Sankai Juku* premiered in Paris in 1982, Amagatsu expressed his homage to prehistory, specifically to the Japanese Jomon era. *Jomon Sho* began with the descent of the four dancers headfirst from the roof of the theater in another reenactment of a birth sequence, which they later performed with great drama both within theaters and outside in public places throughout the world. More recently, Maro returned to his hometown, Nara, the ancient capital city, then danced nearby at Ishii Butai, a famous stone burial chamber overlooking the Asuka plain, where the first Yamato emperors had ruled. The dance was filmed and Maro and his dancers are seen emerging from below the ground, out of the huge rocks of the tomb. They writhe over the ground like Hopi snake dancers rising from their *kiva*, intimate with the earth.

The growth of Butoh has the literal form of Amagatsu's birth drop, a slow unwinding of the human form. It is the descent of the birth passage or the evolution of a culture from its archaic Jomon past. Such origins, like the womb, are of necessity dark. The color of *duende* is black. *Duende*, as defined by Lorca, is the soul that fires the matador, the singer, and the dancer. It springs up through the soles of the feet. Its source is the earth, stretched like a hide across a parched Spain. So, too, Butoh draws its energy from the soil through which the dancers move and from the primordial presence of the ocean. D.H. Lawrence described the Mexican Indians performing the *Dance of the Sprouting Corn* with the same earthy intimacy: "The dancer dances the eternal drooping leap, that brings his life down, down, down, down from the mind, down from the broad, beautiful shaking breast, down to the powerful pivot of the knees, then to the ankles, and plunges deep from the ball of the foot into the earth, towards the earth's red centre, where these men belong, as is signified by the red earth with which they are smeared. . . . And meanwhile the shell cores from the Pacific sway up and down ceaselessly on their breasts."[5]

In 1977 the dancer Min Tanaka traveled the length of Japan, dancing every day, from Kyushu to Hokkaido. On some days he would dance two or three times. His main motive was to feel the difference in the ground at different places. He danced naked and usually outdoors, drawing extreme responses as he continued to improvise. After several arrests he was jailed, and he tried to dance in jail. He called this experiment *Hyperdance*. "I dance not in the place, I dance the place," he said.

Min Tanaka found that the route closest to the influence of Hijikata was to develop a form of dance that was in fact independent and in contrast to Hijikata. He began by dancing naked and his movements were minimal. His body, in superb condition, became a sculptural vehicle. He was an Olympic athlete before he was influenced by ballet and modern dance, so his body had been rigorously disciplined. From his starting point with a form that was almost static, he moved closer and closer to his original inspiration, Hijikata. In 1983 he wrote an homage to Hijikata, who had not danced for ten years, claiming that he was Hijikata's true son. Hijikata read it and indicated that he would dance again in public. His pupil, Yoko Ashikawa, also began to dance again publicly after several years. In 1984, Hijikata choreographed Min Tanaka in a form of dance they called *Love Butoh*, performed to the sound of a tape of Artaud's poem for four voices, xylophone, and percussion, *Pour en finir avec le jugement de Dieu (To Have Done With God's Judgment)*. Artaud made the tape a month before he died in 1948 for Radiodiffusion Française, but the director general banned its broadcast. The tape represents Artaud's scream in its primary and definitive essence. It was one of Hijikata's most precious possessions.

Min Tanaka was surprised at Hijikata's working method. Hijikata would take as many as a thousand images from nature, including elemental forms such as wind and rain, which he would have to remember, then he would apply them throughout Tanaka's body. Hijikata changed their order every day. Only one dancer, Yoko Ashikawa, has the vocabulary of Hijikata's images imprinted on her own memory after working with him for twenty years. Her daily routine would begin with Hijikata beating a small drum and uttering a stream of images like poetry. Without his words she could not dance. He numbered and classified his movements related to the images, so that he literally wrote dance every day.

At one point Hijikata trained Ashikawa to perform as a baby, with a body that was not yet matured. She realized that the training was not designed to mimic, but to enable the dancers to experience their bodies as children, touching, feeling, exploring, and reacting to light. He often used the metaphor of a meal for his dancers, in which their body organs were served up to them on a plate and they would have to pick up their livers, hearts, and lungs and examine them. His dancers, regardless of their origins, unconsciously began to move like children from the north country because they were trained receivers, they had the facility to realize the image. They could be anything, just as the Zen dictum had stated that "to paint bamboo, you must become bamboo." Maro had also said that "Butoh involves a form that almost precedes dance, just as a child moves and plays before he dances."

In 1975, Hijikata's dancers performed *A Rhapsody in Futashimaya*, which began with the image of an infant playing on the floor, rocking his body to and fro, and experimenting with facial expressions. The child was then transformed into a rigid Japanese doll, its fluidity and vitality replaced with immobility. Hijikata choreographed this metamorphosis to Saint-Saëns's *The Swan*, the same music that Michel Fokine had used when he choreographed Anna Pavlova in *The Dying Swan* in 1905. Hijikata had pillaged the popular treasury of ballet, not as a thief, but in perfect correspondence. Both pieces were essential descriptions of death.

His remembrance of childhood was heightened during his period of withdrawal in the early 1970s. When he reappeared in 1974 he wore his hair very long, swept up on the back of his head, in a style that he remembered from his mother and sisters. His sisters had apparently been sold off as children so that the family could survive. The brutal memory was coupled with the realization that their spirits, together with the spirit of his mother, lived inside him and he was feeding them. He answered their spirits by switching sexual identities. "Women are born with the ability to live the illogicality of reality and, as such, they are able to embody the illogicality of dancing," he said, uttering in a similar breath, reminiscent of his friend Mishima, "Japanese men have been emasculated by the West."[6]

The aging of Hijikata parallels a counter-movement back to the source, to the earth and the feminine. "Butoh is created in the mother's womb as life is, and its energy and mechanism should be the same," wrote Kazuo Ohno. "The world of Butoh must be that of the mother's womb."

Ohno's dance is centered on creation and the life cycle. He has been a Christian for more than fifty years and he has absorbed the Christian cycle of birth, pain, death, and resurrection into his own creative perspective. His performances in the Holy Land and his visit to the shores of the Dead Sea have intensified and clarified his vision. "Jesus was a Butoh master," he claimed. He danced the *Call of Jesus* in a church at Nancy in France and realized, "The church was a womb. The steps had been worn away by time. I felt my mother's womb and crouched and sank." In 1981, Hijikata directed Ohno in the latter's dance, *My Mother*, which opened with *A Dream of the Fetus*. Ohno was seventy-five years old.

I was in Ohno's studio on a hillside overlooking Yokohama recently. He talked about the Dead Sea and about the universality of his work. He was completing a grueling international schedule. He excitedly produced a postcard of a tomb he had recently visited in Milan. It showed two reclining figures of *Santi Gervaso e Protaso* in the Basilica di Sant' Ambrogio. He had returned to the tomb several times, fascinated by the sculptured figures of the dead, which reminded him of Jesus and the Virgin Mary. After dancing in the studio for nearly two hours, improvising around *La Argentina*, he began a new piece with different makeup. Pointing to the white flower he was holding, he said, "My mother." Then pointing to the only other prop, a small red table, "My mother," he repeated.

Butoh is at once both universal and intensely Japanese, just as Tokyo, a city unto itself, becomes the model for *The City*, when we imagine the metropolis of the future. Tokyo is the zone of crossed wires, where culture is consumed and transformed from all global sources to create a culture that is very specifically a product of the zone. One of Hijikata's last pieces of choreography for Yoko Ashikawa was *Sakura a La España* (*Spanish Cherry*, 1983). The Spanish flavor was added to the clichéd symbol of the Japanese spring. This is a cocktail art, in which the world can be mixed and relocalized, yet the hybrid is what makes this art both contemporary and timeless. Butoh bursts out onto the world stage in the company of the new German Expressionist dance of Pina Bausch. It is appropriate, however, that a culture that has no convention of the nude in the history of its art should also provide a climate where Leni Riefenstahl's photographs of the Nuba are adored, and where the bodybuilder Lisa Lyon becomes an instrument in the hands of the graphic virtuoso, Tadanori Yokoo.

Butoh at its worst remains pure spectacle, which the West, in its own greed for exotic distraction, will consume and forget. But Butoh in its pure form transcends its own history, born out of the dark postnuclear years of a devastated Japan. With an echo of Artaud's primal scream, Butoh knocks down the door of all safely packaged, over-mediated art for complacent consumption. Butoh is an art that lives dangerously.

In a Tokyo basement, at an experimental performance laboratory, I saw Min Tanaka perform *Viola*, an extract from *Der violetter Vorhang* (*The Violet Curtain*, 1914), an outline by Wassily Kandinsky that Min Tanaka had choreographed and performed at the 1984 Venice Biennale. Two men and two women, in black jackets, mouths open, and their eyes rolling, advanced in a shuffle across the darkened room toward the audience. They twisted their bodies in blind embraces. It was an image of the blind leading the blind. Sweat dripped from their faces and no sound emerged. It was the silent scream. At times the dancers looked like a sculptural frieze in some monumental but morbid statuary. They sometimes jerked spasmodically like Hijikata in *Revolt of the Flesh*. From out of the audience Min Tanaka advanced in a long coat, spitting arcs of white rice from his mouth, to be ravaged by the two women, naked except for men's shoes. At the climax of the dance, one of the women screamed and the silence which separated the action from the viewer was broken.

Although the source was Kandinsky, the form of the dance was apocalyptic and postnuclear, employing imagery, like the retreat of the blinded, which only the Japanese have experienced so directly. Within Japan, such a performance can exist only in the subterranean laboratory. Regardless of its presence on the international stage, Butoh is vital as long as it remains on the periphery of Japanese culture, where its danger and Artaudian rebellion are not quietened. The acceptance of Hijikata as a great artist began with his death in 1986. Butoh is now a culturally exportable commodity, yet it also exists as a critical challenge to the materialism of the society from which it was spawned. The very recognition it has for so long deserved potentially threatens its life, though the influence of Butoh will be indefinite.

Hijikata's own course completes a cycle. Blown like the wind from the icy north into the midst of a city of economic recovery, gross national product figures, and robotic factory floors, he found the Tohoku inside himself and released it. Shortly before his death he danced in the film *Makiko Monogatari* (*Makiko's Story*, 1986), in which he appears as the custodian of a small shrine for *Kannon*, the Buddhist Mother Goddess, the Goddess of Mercy. He is a Fool like the figure of *Kamaitachi*. He talks to the statue, which he loves and eventually carries off. In a double suicide he disappears into the river with *Kannon* in his arms.

After transforming the possibilities of his art, Hijikata retreated further into his memory of childhood. With innocence he advanced into infancy. On his deathbed, surrounded by those who had come to pay tribute, he sat up and danced his ultimate performance, conscious of his losses, of the things that were slipping away, and of what was given to others, as a sacrifice of sorts.

1. Nario Goda, "Tatsumi Hijikata, Japan's Avant-Garde Dancer," NHK Broadcast, August 1976   2. Ibid.   3. Ibid.   4. Martin Esslin, *Antonin Artaud*, Fontana, London, 1976   5. D.H. Lawrence, *Mornings in Mexico*, Martin Secker, London, 1927   6. Nario Goda, "Tatsumi Hijikata, Japan's Avant-Garde Dancer," NHK Broadcast, August 1976

I met Hijikata in 1966 when I was nineteen years old, and shortly afterwards I began to work with him. I was an art student studying painting before I met him, I was not a dancer. Maybe after two years of working with him, he realized that I was a serious disciple of his.

I remember the preparations for his performance of *Revolt of the Flesh* in 1968. For about a year before the performance there was a strong feeling that Hijikata was withdrawing into a period of isolation or introspection. A month before, Hijikata prepared his body with a strict diet. He drank just milk and a little weak *miso*, but no tea. He went running every day, even on the hottest days. He also exposed his skin to artificial lights in order to get a deep tan. He wore no makeup during the performance. The long-term preparation involved physical training, fasting, and being alone and avoiding any association with other people. Only at the end of his preparation did he concern himself with the staging of the performance. The idea of raising himself on ropes at the climax came only at the end of his planning.

The fascination for me was that he was thirty-nine years old at the time and his body was in superb condition. In the course of a two-hour performance, he started as a thirty-nine year old, and gradually he became younger and younger. He became thirty-five, then he was twenty-five, eighteen, twelve, and I remember thinking there must be a secret. This must be the secret of dance.

The responses were extreme. Those who didn't like it, felt they had been made to see something they did not want to see, something offensive. They may have felt that they were being attacked or scolded from the stage.

After *Revolt of the Flesh*, one phase of Hijikata's work was completed. After 1970 he embarked on his life's work, which still continues now after his death. There is a big division between these two phases. There was a feeling of liberation from 1970 when he entered a new, unexplored territory. He was going to become more like a child, not through reviving his childhood memories, but by starting something new. It was from this period that he decided not to think too much, but to be more like a child, with less concern for self-identification. He then began to work in this way with his students.

There was a conscious effort in his training to reconstruct a child's wisdom, a kind of innocence which children possess, which we have forgotten, especially in regard to their bodies. He used the metaphor of a meal for dancers served on a plate, on which were placed the dancer's liver, lungs, and heart. The plate was wide and shallow, and the dancer was encouraged to play with the organs and examine them. This is something that children do unconsciously; they play with parts of their bodies in order to recognize them. He was constantly encouraging his students to explore in this way. He would often say, "Let your hand do this," or "Let your leg do this," in contrast to the usual designated function of the limb.

He choreographed for me dances that were based on puppets or babies, for bodies that were not yet mature. Looking back, I understand that his training was not designed to mimic puppets or babies, but to enable the dancers to really experience, not just as a training routine, but to realize their bodies like a baby, through touching, feeling, or exploring. This was the basis of his choreography.

Hijikata needed a recipient. I had to be very receptive, and his demands were physically very extreme. For almost ten years our daily routine began with his drumming on a small drum stretched with animal hide, rather like a Buddhist drum, and with his words, which he uttered in a stream like poetry. When we danced, the images were all derived from his verbal expression. Without the words we could not dance, so it was like following a poem. He very much liked to number and classify his movements according to the images. I have been working so long with these images that it is very difficult to single them out. He was creating images all the time. He literally *wrote* dance. Recently I was surprised to hear him say, "Writers can write as much as one hundred pages

YOKO ASHIKAWA

Dance: Intimacy Plays Its Trump

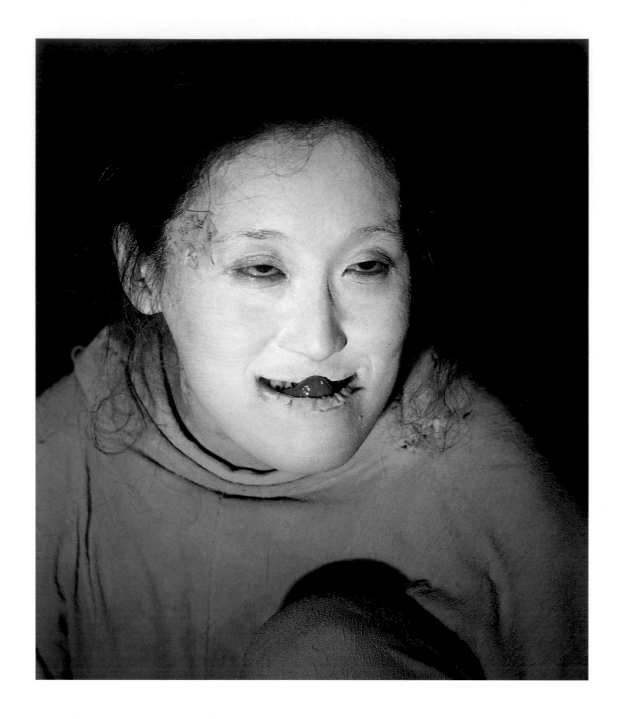

a day. It's so much. They can write like I work. Isn't that surprising?" He was surprised at the similarities between writers' creative processes and his own. I am hesitant, however, to describe him as a great genius, or to create a myth about him, because I have to continue his endeavors, and work closely with his vocabulary and system which I have inherited. If I described him as too much of a myth, then it would be impossible for me to continue on my own.

The details of my childhood are very different from Hijikata's Tohoku experience. I was born in Chiba and lived in Tokyo. When I trained to dance like a baby, the one thing that was most important to me was to explore and find the light. The child reacts to light, the experience is common to babies anywhere. Hijikata's dancers, regardless of whether they were brought up in the city or suburbia, without any direct observation, unconsciously began to move like children from the north country, from Tohoku. In any dance there are hundreds of elements or fragments, which can be encoded and retrieved to make one piece. Their origins might be with a child from the north, but if the dancer is a good receiver and has the physical facility to realize the image, then the dancer can be anything regardless of his or her personal origins. To get to that point of

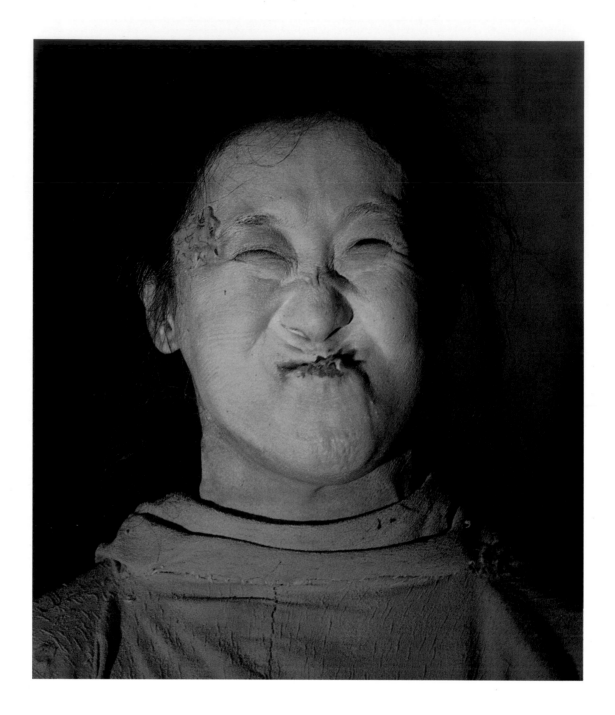

versatility, the dancer does not have to impose an experience of the north or go through any kind of psychoanalytical process. Perhaps for Hijikata there was some kind of proto-blank state, but because I had no equivalent state, I could take on any state at all.

Hijikata reached a stage when he said he would no longer perform or work alone. He gave so much to the executor of his work, who served as the recipient. I was not simply the instrument; there was no separation between the player and the instrument. Our relationship was symbiotic.

I realize that I still have to rid myself of self-centered feelings. Hijikata was not involved with me alone. He worked on the dance with many individuals and was totally involved with each one. Now I am going to immerse myself in his work, in his world. Now that he is no longer here physically, he has to come back somewhere. When he was here he had nothing; coming back here, he has nothing, he is alone. He realized that he could not be alone and continue dancing, so he found more people *within himself*. Even though he was working with many dancers, he was working with many dancers *within himself*. That was his art. Now I have to take that feeling out to my real body. That is something I have to find myself.

YOKO ASHIKAWA, 1986, Tokyo

20

Our petrified idea of the theater is connected with our petrified idea of a culture without shadows, where, no matter which way it turns, our mind *(esprit)* encounters only emptiness, though space is full.

But the true theater, because it moves and makes use of living instruments, continues to stir up shadows where life has never ceased to grope its way. The actor does not make the same gestures twice, but he makes gestures, he moves; and although he brutalizes forms, nevertheless behind them and through their destruction he rejoins that which outlives forms and produces their continuation.

The theater, which is in *no thing*, but makes use of everything—gestures, sounds, words, screams, light, darkness—rediscovers itself at precisely the point where the mind requires a language to express its manifestations.

ANTONIN ARTAUD
The Theater and Culture,
The Theater and Its Double, 1938

DAI RAKUDA KAN
Dance: The North Sea

When I was in the mountains which surround the Dead Sea, I turned toward the sun and I felt that the movement of the continental shelves, which has been going on since the world was created, was reflected in the depths of my heart. In this Buto space, which the Dead Sea represents, I heard, out of nowhere, a requiem which engulfed me. Facing the sun I allowed everything I possessed to slip away. . . . It was an infinite movement. I heard great things, comparable to the Sermon on the Mount, but I did not realize it.

I thought that no beast could live in such a place, so I was surprised when I saw innumerable animals running over the mountains. They looked like weasels and they jumped around the sun-charred slopes making a lot of noise. Their cries resounded across the universe like an immense choir. Death, birth, life, all of this is the same.

Mankind has a story as does the cosmos. Superimposed on the story of the cosmos, man's story unfolds. Within this cosmological superimposition emerges the path that leads from birth through maturity to death. The Butoh costume is like throwing the cosmos onto one's shoulders. And for Butoh, while the costume covers the body, it is the body that is the costume of the soul.

A fetus walked along a snow-covered path. It cleared a path by spreading its clothes upon the snow after removing them one by one as in a secret cosmic ceremony. Then it peeled off its skin and laid that upon the path. A whirlwind of snow surrounded it, but the fetus continued, wrapped in this whirlwind. The white bones danced, enveloped by an immaculate cloak. This dance of the fetus, which moved along as if carried by the whirlwind of snow, seemed to be transparent.

In life there is, without a doubt, something beyond the brashness of youth which bursts like summer light. There is something between life and death. This part of ourselves is like the wreck of an abandoned car; if we fix it, it could start up again.

Simply thinking about it sets my heart beating. Butoh's best moment is the moment of extreme weariness when we make a supreme effort to overcome exhaustion. That reminds me of my show in Caracas. I was covered in sweat. My body had grown old and I was working like a rickety old car, but I was happy. Is that what we call wearing oneself out for glory?

The dead begin to run.

KAZUO OHNO
Extracts from *The Dead Begin to Run*

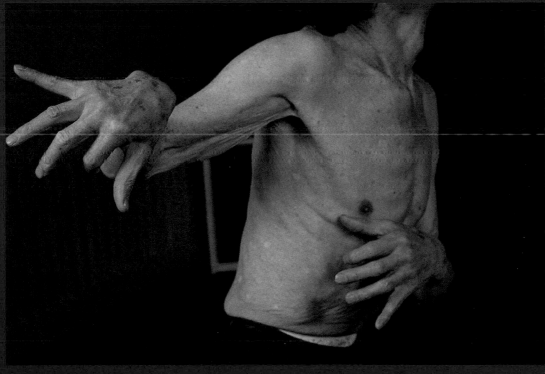

KAZUO OHNO
Dance: Admiring La Argentina

The dance of La Argentina, Antonia Mercé, which I saw from the third floor of the Imperial Theater in 1928, was an unforgettable encounter. During the subsequent fifty years the vision returned now and again. But no matter if I called her or cried for her, she never appeared in front of me again, though she hid deep in my soul.

At the opening of a show by the painter Natsuyuki Nakanishi in 1976, I walked into the gallery and was nailed in front of a painting. *"La Argentina!"* I thought. I finally met her in that painting. Nakanishi had never seen her dance, and had probably never heard of her. I don't know why I recognized her in that particular painting, but after this reunion with La Argentina, I was determined to perform on stage again and in 1977 I gave a performance entitled *Admiring La Argentina.*

The dance of La Argentina invited people to a sea of excitement. She embodied dance, literature, music, and art, and furthermore she represented love and pain in real life. She would have said, "It was not my art that moved people. I simply received all things that moved me as they were, and I try to pass them to you. I am simply a servant conveying these things to you."

KAZUO OHNO

38

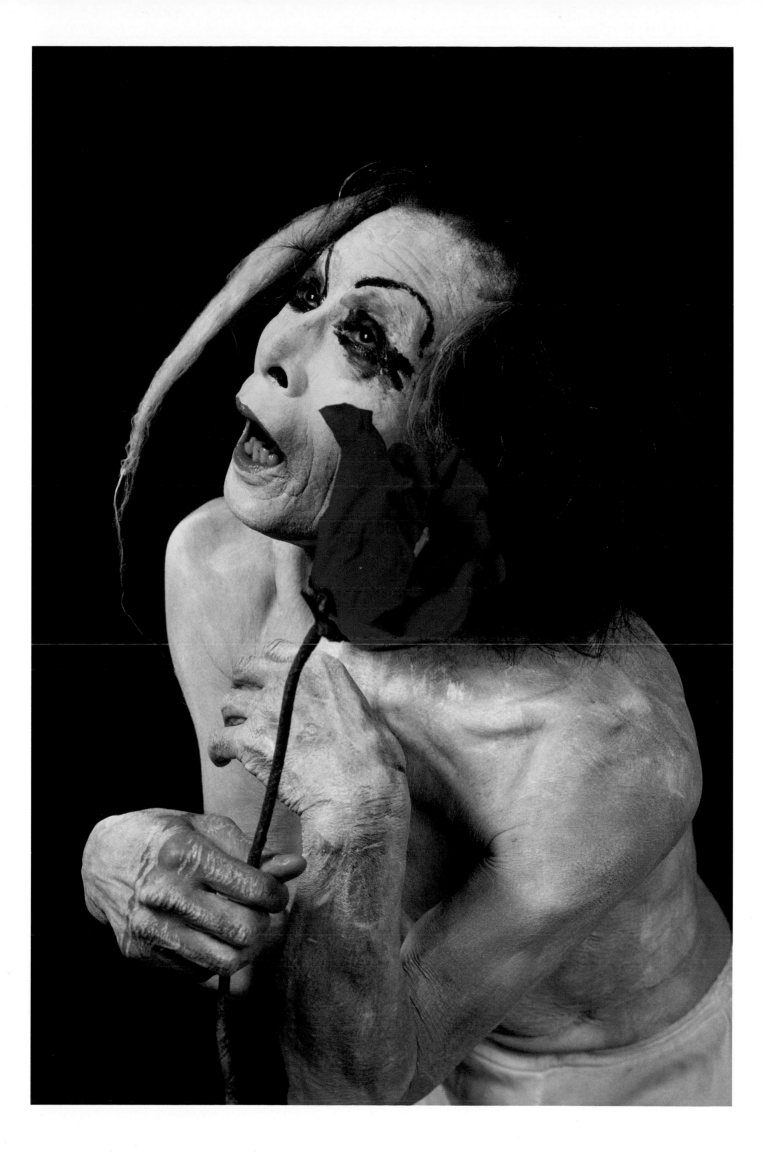

We live with our bodies, and perceive the world, by keeping the eyes of our bodies open.

The birthplace of our emotion, too, manifested its existence through these body-eyes.

The mysterious tradition of the body attracts my attention, as much as I am preoccupied with myself.

This body—the environment called "me"—is encircled by time: It is the world.

This body lives with the inevitable molecular tradition, and it ages in apparent ambivalence.

The world—the external environment—and the body—the internal environment—each try to establish a style, when they encounter each other, on the basis of their respective traditions.

The tradition of the body is constantly exposed to the will for transformation, and it dances the eternal time—awkward, twisted, and suffering.

Avant-garde is a rebellious love for time.

Dance is a humble determination.

It is a will to struggle, so that the self remains open-ended in its relation to the world.

Since many years ago, I have been thinking there would be no time, till I die, that I can use for myself.

It does not mean that I am living for the sake of others;

I am living for my own sake.

But since I want to live myself to the fullest, there is not "I" or "me."

When a person becomes conscious of "self," he realizes that this living organism "I" has been a collection of pieces from the very moment of its birth.

Thus, we must say, we are not really born yet.

We are imperfect forever.

It is even what I wish to be—my will to be.

I will never be mature.

To wish to be mature is a silly thing, I think.

There must be a revolution which, people always consider, has not started yet.

It is an incessant revolution—without a pause.

It is revolution which one never thinks about.

MIN TANAKA
Extracts from Tradition of the Body and Dance Avant-Garde

MIN TANAKA
WITH MAI JUKU
Dance: Daytime Moon

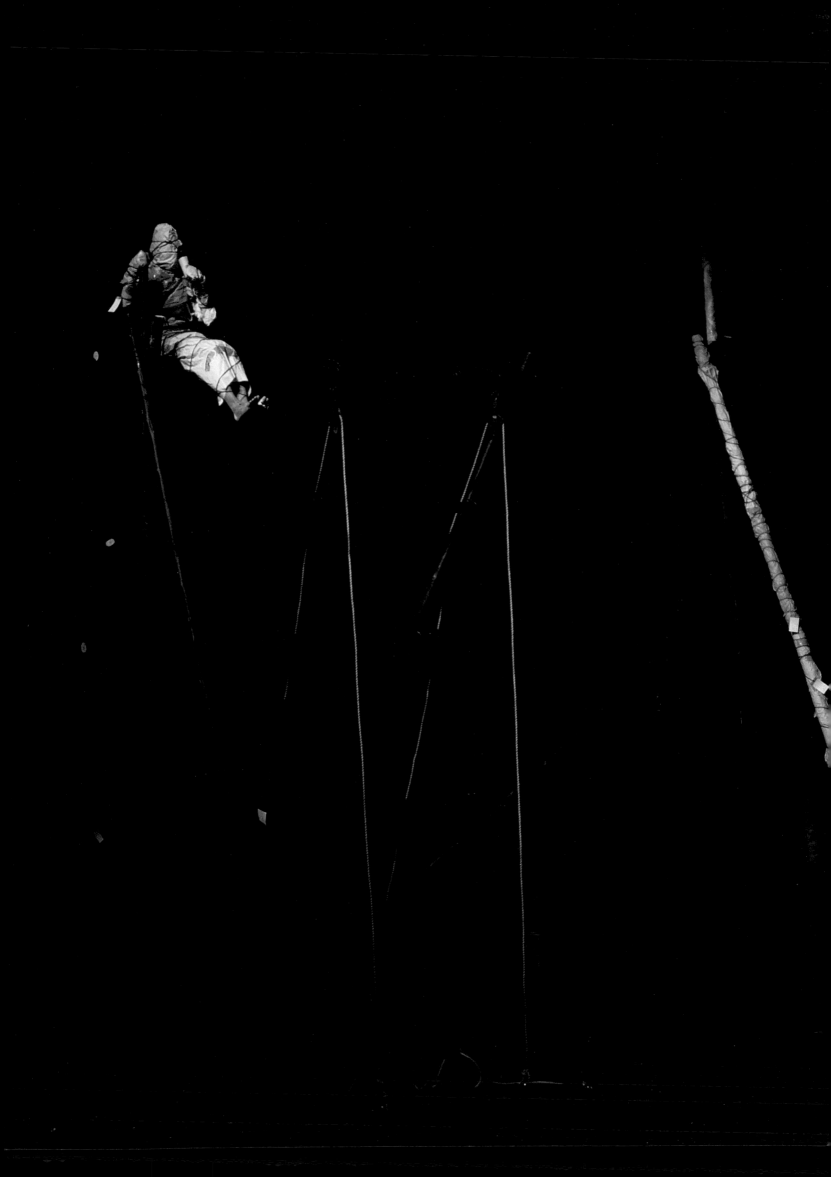

If I were a sculptor, I might say that watching Min Tanaka dance taught me a great deal about sculpture. Since I am a writer, I will propose that I learned an amazing amount in a short time about the movements of insects, of plants, and of animals, was introduced to the inner life of a baby beginning to walk and saw the flights of pterodactyls, and the sleep of the dead.

NORMAN MAILER

In the daytime you can sometimes still see the moon. A long time ago when I was twenty, I was digging a well. One day, in the very deep hole, I could see the reflection of the moon. My head was very clear at the time and I had a sense of total comprehension.

The dancers are insects under a tree watching the moon. The wooden frames are used for drying rice straws, or for hanging *daikon*, and they have different names in different districts. I like them when they have been weathered after being left out for a long time. Then they look like bones. The figures wrapped in paper are presents to the world. They are covered with the names of many cities throughout the world. I want to send them to many parts of the world. There were many dancers in the group from all over the world. I was sending them back.

MIN TANAKA

I AM AN AVANT-GARDE WHO CRAWLS THE EARTH
HOMAGE TO TATSUMI HIJIKATA

By Min Tanaka

I have not seen a landscape in Tatsumi Hijikata's dance. I am an avant-garde who crawls the Earth, a corpse trying desperately to become life in the circle of life and death. The surface of the body dances from one neighbor to another, toward another house which will be the next locus. The body that revenges the sight, the invisible dance that destroys visible phantasm. Hijikata's fingers are always concrete. Phantasm emerges only when a body does not fight and demands a house. I am an avant-garde who crawls the Earth. The structure of the body resists the society and its functions raise a fist toward the world.

Hijikata is a body who was born from an authentic operation to make the body remain as it is. This body comes close to us even when it jumps behind for 100 kilometers. Butoh (dance) is not the dance of the epoch. It is said that Butoh was the manifestation of a desire for metamorphosis. But I don't think so. Butoh engaged itself in a combat with a painted body, but the body remained raw. Tatsumi Hijikata longed for nothing. Ankoku Butoh (darkness dance) is a joyous despair. The body does not exist unless one is astonished with its ingenuous state.

I have not seen a landscape in Tatsumi Hijikata's dance. To put judgment out of order, to disorder respiration, to forget the purpose, not to respond to comprehension, to exchange the subject and the object, and to crystallize with shame. Didn't you want to get up, seeing Tatsumi Hijikata standing up? But were you not trapped in aesthetics when you saw him so thin and weakened?

I am an avant-garde who crawls the Earth. To be naked was for me a way to dress up myself. To abandon judgment was for me a combat. As Tatsumi Hijitaka never wanted to dance without a public, I aspired to dance only in the presence of other people. Because dance is essentially somebody else's business. To evacuate one's own body, to step into obscure region of matter, to rush to other people's important matters. Or, to constantly steal sensations, and to involve others in a chaotic dance of the mind. Or to flip off the world as if it were a band tied around your head.

For seven years I used my limbs only as tools to sustain my body. I used to regard the hands as a banal language. I used to refuse everyday speed to outgrow my physical size. I was conscious of the speed of other people's thoughts, for I wanted to know if the dance is born before or after the thought. I was dancing so slowly that it was almost invisible. I wished to become alert quietly, very quietly.

Somebody said dance is something that visits us. But preoccupied about the structure of the body, I politely abstained from the advent of the dance. I turned around my palm toward it saying, "Just a moment, please." The speed of thought, of nerves, of blood circulation, of muscular tissues, of the spirit; the chaotic coexistence of various speeds made me excited and alert. I lay down everywhere and the combat still continues.

Hijikata told me one day: "You are a man of flesh." Yes, I am a man of flesh with a gear capable of ten different speeds. I lie down anywhere with my eyes half open. The flesh does not know the landscape nor the history. It starts with nothing but being flesh. The body surface that envelops the flesh is like a wrapping paper; and what is important is the pattern printed on it. The patterns of the society are inevitably printed on the body surface as it rolls around on the Earth. The dance permeated the body surface and reached the flesh. My body was turned into a receptacle.

I am an avant-garde who crawls the Earth, a body that possesses a language. The language lives in symbiosis with the functions of the body. Dance emerges between bodies. The experience of thoughts erects the dance. Did Hijikata deliver words, or did he devour them? Hijikata stirred up words. That's how my flesh remembers. When words are stirred up and erect themselves, the body trembles and recalls phantasmagoric movements. By the way, do words turn into landscape?

Our speeds are controlled by the world. Hijikata initiated a movement that would never arrive at the destination in order to counterattack controlled speeds. As for me, I took on a speed by abandoning speed. The deviation and discontinuous equilibrium of the body for destroying the order of time. The stable immobility like abandoned slippers. The deformity of the body that tackles down words. The sedimentation like that which occurs when we oddly run into somebody on a slope. The image emits high fever and makes the wind blow. Hijikata's back was bitten by the winds.

I have not seen a landscape in Tatsumi Hijikata's dance. The irritation of having an idea stings the future in his dance. The body repeats promises carefully in order to break them. Hijikata as he is in whom the optimistic sorrow can travel to anywhere. I knew beforehand that, even if Hijikata showed me the landscape, it would be a defeat called "culture" for me to acknowledge it. That is why I still have a hangover.

I am a swan returning north, I am an avant-garde who crawls the Earth. An optimistic intuition inspired by any given field I find myself in discovers the advent of dance in the course of Earth's history which is also the history of our spirit. If we have profound individualities, it would not be too bad that disorder might prevail several hundred years later. But it may be necessary that there be ephemeral and delicate hierarchy. Emotion is useful for the recognition of hierarchy. For it is believed to be a private property. History has been controlling emotions of all kinds, but I shall write about the phenomenon someday. The problem is to know where nostalgia situates itself.

One may define Hijikata as the manifestation of the kind of emotion one cannot possess exclusively. From the very beginning, Hijikata was an emotion, and the genealogy of the body never rested on individual nostalgia. Love clenches the teeth and makes the buttocks tremble. My actual work is to awaken emotions of the body sleeping in the depth of history. It is not necessary to accentuate the presence of the dancer. Ring the bell inside the body and become a receptacle trying to remain erect with oblique eyes. Hijikata seems to eat winds. There is no question about it. Viscera that cannot even eat winds would never be able to becalm words.

I have never seen a landscape in Tatsumi Hijikata's dance. Things never stop moving. We know how to invent a way to move. Above all, we know how to slide laterally—a very terrestrial way to move. I was often fascinated by Hijikata's trick: to slide laterally by moving the axis. I like his very intense expression to move his body as if he were turning around his palms very carefully. Neither modern nor primitive: the two at the same time. The surface of the body dances from one neighbor to another, toward an unknown house which will be the next locus.

I am an avant-garde who crawls the Earth. Since January of 1982, I have been giving a title to my dance: "Emotion." It is an experience to encounter the body, the most authentic body for me. I carry slowly a bucket filled with water. I scream to the water in the bucket. I carry a pickaxe on my shoulder, pound the floor with my feet repeatedly, and cry to the distance "Not yet? Not yet?"

I stare at my body as though looking might bore through it. I touch, lick, bite, pinch, beat, tear, and rub my body. I press a sickle onto my eyelids, grab my penis, rub my belly, and make it swell. When I accumulate hundreds of simple acts of this sort, I feel sad not knowing why. I get divided. I observe. One should also fight against words. I am about to forget about whom I must talk.

I am also engaged in a secret operation so that I will not be eaten up by the society. Since 1976 I have chosen to use the word *Shin-tai* (mind-body) rather than *Niku-tai* (flesh-body) to describe body. *Shintai* seems to have opened a wider world to me. But it also seems that it has robbed me partly of the force to support myself. I envisage the coexistence of flesh and mind. It will be my duty for myself to mix the two in a manner comprehensible to anybody.

I have not seen a landscape in Tatsumi Hijikata's dance. The body created things and sold out landscape. Since Hijikata stung my eyes, I became his son. I am still intensely irritated. I wish to become an artist who shoots an arrow to everyday life. Hijikata constantly whispers strategy into my ears, and I would like to introduce him to all of you hardly standing on enfeebled legs.

But please be careful not to become an easy-going fan. Butoh will be born between you and Hijikata the moment you are possessed by an insolent ambition. Lastly, I would like to declare that Min Tanaka is a legitimate son of Tatsumi Hijikata.

(Translated by Kazue Kobata)

I was very influenced by Hijikata, but I did not want to go to him. I decided to go my own way. Hijikata had stopped dancing for ten years and I really wanted him to dance again in public. In 1983 I wrote an homage to him which he read, and he came to see me. We talked and he decided he would dance again in public.

In 1984 I decided I would ask him if I could work with him. I wasn't part of the Butoh mainstream. I had kept my own way of dancing. I was favored by Hijikata and I felt that I had to study with him, so I asked him to choreograph me. He agreed and we worked together for two months. I was very surprised by his way of working. He used about a thousand images from nature applied throughout the body, and I had to remember every one. Each day he changed the order of the movements. The images were of such elements as wind or sunshine, and he used them not to provide form, but to provide the inspiration. The movements were natural. It was a great experience. No personality was involved in the choreography. The piece we developed had no name, but we used it as the basis for a form we called *Love Butoh*, because it was based on our association. The sound we used was from a rare tape of Antonin Artaud.

When I first began dancing, even if I moved my body a lot, I couldn't dance unless I had some real feeling. I decided never to dance without feeling. I realized that the feeling was outside my body, and I thought I might be able to get the feeling into my body. At the time, people talked about dance coming from the inside, but I thought the dance had to come from outside and meet inside. I knew from a young age that my spirit was outside, and I was deeply ashamed to go down deep within my body. I wanted to go deep outside my body.

Little by little over a period of seven years my dance has changed from its slow naked form, so that now I dance with clothes, like this raincoat, which is like skin, or with paper. Recently I have been wearing a raincoat, ex-Italian army issue, and a black suit. Hijikata always said I was a *dancing soldier*.

MIN TANAKA, 1986, Tokyo

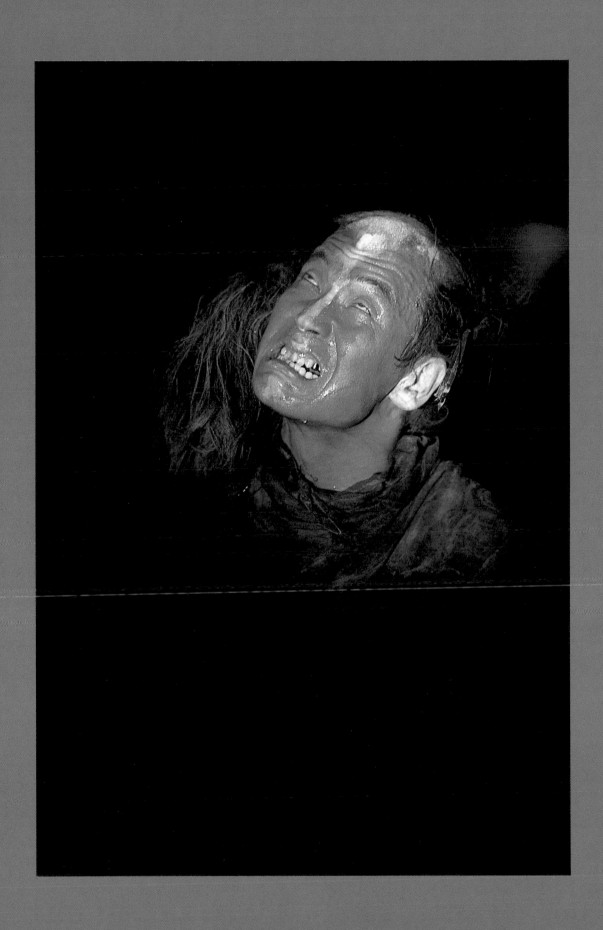

MIN TANAKA
Dance: Foundation of Love Butoh

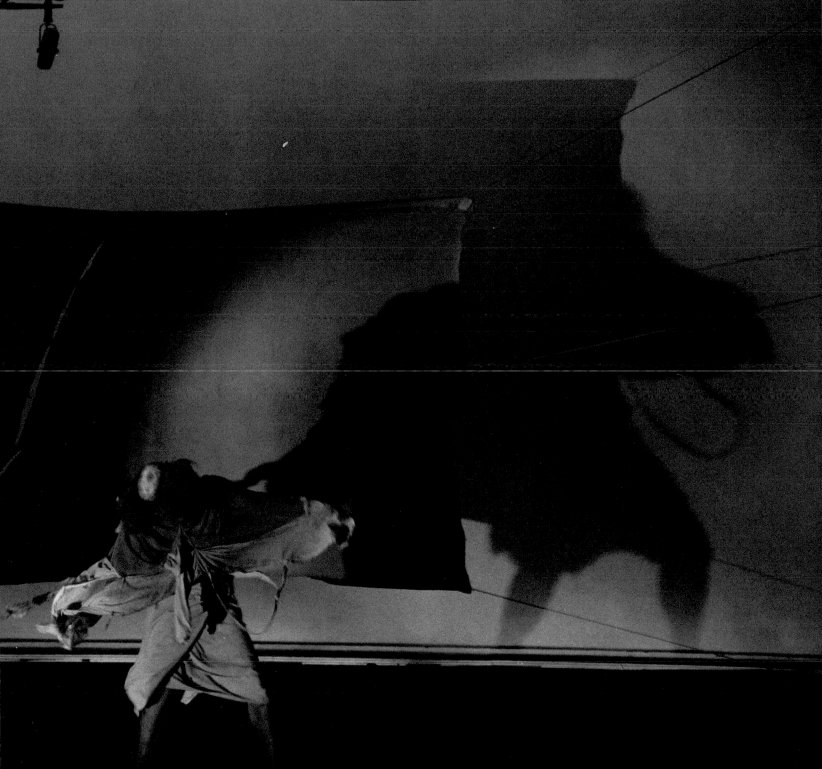

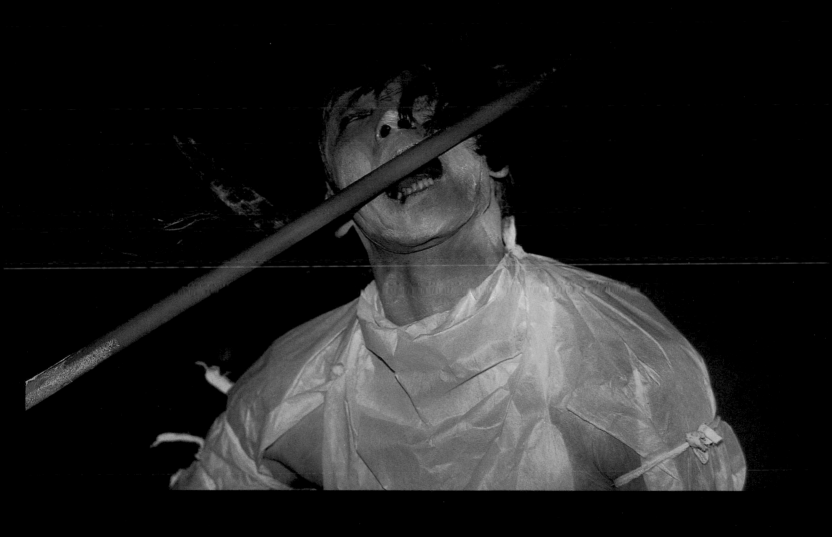

I lived with Hijikata for about three years from 1965. I was nineteen and he was in his mid-thirties. I came to live at his house like a stray cat. At my first meeting with him I had a strong sense of my own past, my roots. He was a country person living in Tokyo, and I was from Nara, which was just a quiet town, but it was the end of the Silk Route, so it was somewhere very special.

Hijikata used the term Butoh to describe his dance. Although modern dance is something that is liberated from Western classical dance, Butoh is not comparable. If modern dance is like a thoroughbred racehorse, then Butoh is like a camel. The difference is like the difference between diamonds and cork, though both have the same elemental base.

Butoh is just a Japanese name. There are many parallel dances elsewhere. When I first saw *Omizutori*, the fire festival on the hillside at Nara, an ancient religious ceremony from the eleventh century, the ceremony seemed like an imitation of my dance, just as I may have drawn from an eleventh century ritual. I was very impressed by the age of the ritual. Butoh is something new, but there are many comparable forms throughout history. Butoh is a form that almost precedes dance, just as a child moves and plays before he dances.

Butoh is also like *Haiyatomai*, another ancient dance form that would follow the fighting between rival clans. The losers would dance the *Haiyatomai* for the winners. Like flamenco, Butoh draws its energy from the earth. The style is different, but the concept is the same. Butoh also comes out of a specific Japanese culture, and out of a Japanese avant-garde.

Imagine a snake emerging and appearing before a Japanese farmer, then sliding away. The step with which the farmer may have crushed the snake, may have been the beginning of a Butoh step.

I founded *Dai Rakuda Kan* in 1972. Hijikata encouraged me to be independent. The first time he saw *Dai Rakuda Kan* he didn't like it. The second time, he recognized that I was following a different and independent course and he accepted it. It was the aim of *Dai Rakuda Kan* to add dynamism and drama to Butoh, to enlarge the spectacle. *Dai Rakuda Kan*, meaning literally *Great Camel Battleship*, carries the spirit of the lion, the camel, and the baby. Hijikata was the strength of the lion, while the camel represented endurance and the baby innocence. In the Chinese horoscope there is no camel, so the camel combines all the good qualities of the other animals. The camel is somewhere between a mythical animal and a real animal. It is also the animal that crossed the Silk Route.

In Japan there is a great materialism and a great contradiction in people's attitude toward nature. If the unique economic situation in contemporary Japan is described as a miracle, then Butoh is another Japanese miracle; it is the antithesis of the economic miracle and it is a total rejection of the values of that materialism. We need to stop the accelerated activity of development. We need to block the velocity. Butoh is therefore a dangerous force. The way of Butoh is dangerous.

AKAJI MARO, 1986, Tokyo

AKAJI MARO
Dance: Solo from Book of Five Rings

The theater is neither a set of facilities nor a building. It is the *ideology* of a place where dramatic encounters are created.

Any place can become a theatrical space. At the same time, if no drama develops there, a theater may simply become part of the landscape of daily life.

Those of us who consider ourselves dramatists take it as crucial to be able to organize our imaginations in such a way as to change any location into a theater.

In the view of the Tenjosajiki group, to reflect upon theater is to reflect upon the city.

The theory of the theater is also that of the urban community and its topography.

The place is not just a geographical occasion. It is also a historically rooted structure dependent upon specific, indigenous traditions.

SHUJI TERAYAMA, from "Manifesto,"
The Drama Review, December 1985

The name *Byakko-sha* refers literally to *White Tiger's Company*. There are several images associated with it. During the Meiji Restoration there was a group of young men called *Byakkotai* associated with the *Bakufu*, the Tokugawa government, that was attacked by some sea forces. The group consisted entirely of fifteen-year-olds who tried in vain to defend the castle. These youths finally escaped and collectively committed suicide by *seppuku*. These fifteen-year-olds possessed both courage and a kind of innocence. The name *Byakko-sha* is derived from the name of this group.

There is also the image of the tiger in your body, which is the spiritual song of your ancestors which sleeps in your body. At the right opportunity the song that is sleeping in your body awakens, going wild like a tiger and it can awaken violently just like a sleeping child raised out of sleep.

I was born in Hiroshima in January 1946 just after the bomb was dropped. My parents were radiation victims, they are certified *hibakusha*. When I was small they told me about the experience. I remember they said the glass in the windows was first purple, then blue, then pink, then it exploded. Perhaps owing to this experience it is color that first impresses me whenever I come to the unfamiliar places.

I came to Tokyo in 1968, at the time of rioting and demonstrations in Shinjuku and Shibuya. In response to this climate there was tremendous physical expression through street theater and performance. Once in the early seventies I took part in a performance in Shibuya in which someone was actually hanged for six seconds. The rope was cut and he fell as his body, which I received, was already turning stiff. He sympathized with Mishima's theme that the body is made anew when the spirit is enlarged to the limit.

The name *Ankoku Butoh* was originally used to refer to the dance of Hijikata and Ohno. They were interested in Western and Japanese dance. I was interested in Asian dance. Hijikata was born in Tohoku, and Ohno in Hokkaido. Both were from the far north of Japan. I am from the South, which is completely different. Whereas their dance might be *Tohokukabuki*, my performance is *Asiankabuki*. Unlike the South, Tohoku is a very cold and dark place as *Ankoku* implies. Japan, like Indonesia, is not a single country or a single culture; there are great differences between North and South. In Japan there is a tendency to categorize, so all this work, however diverse, is called *Butoh*. Butoh seems to have been originated in the sixties under the influence of Surrealism, Dada, and literature, almost in the atmosphere of a secret society. Our dance is developing in the eighties through street performance so that even the passersby become spectators. Ankoku Butoh cut out all superfluous elements, and tried to reduce and concentrate its effects, whereas we try to make our stage by gathering together all genres such as music, visual imagery, the body, costumes, and so on. Then "the body as the infectious media" occurs in contrast to the closed body, which tended to be kept secret in the sixties.

In Southeast Asia it is possible for the Japanese to recognize their Asian identity, but Europe remains a foreign place. When we performed in Bali it was like being at home, or like seeing what Japan might once have been.

One of the differences between the traditional arts somewhere in Southeast Asia, like Bali, and in Japan, is that in Japan there is a clear difference between musicians or performers and amateur performers such as farmers. In Bali this is not true; in the daytime you find men out fishing or working in the fields, then at night they put on their makeup and suddenly begin to dance as artists, and then they change back again into their everyday roles. Bali, with its constant sense of potential theater and an innovative tradition, impressed me more than any other place in Southeast Asia. The leader of the village in Bali where we were staying was called Mandara. He said that our performances had something common with the trance dance known as *San Gyan*, which was popular before Hindu culture entered Bali Island from Java.

ISAMU OHSUKA

BYAKKO-SHA
Dance: Skylark and Lying Buddha

I read a text by Kandinsky describing his ideas for a piece called *Viola*, which was never performed, and I decided to choreograph it. We created a name for each movement of the performance. The opening movement is called *The Crying Wall*, which is followed by *Dead Branches*. In his text Kandinsky refers to a *Violet Night* on a horse, which I danced. My concept, which I applied continually, was that time did not progress like a ladder through a sequence, but that all time coexisted at the same moment.

MIN TANAKA

In the Oriental theater of metaphysical tendencies, as opposed to the Occidental theater of psychological tendencies, this whole complex of gestures, signs, postures, and sonorities which constitute the language of stage performance, this language which develops all its physical and poetic effects on every level of consciousness and in all senses, necessarily induces thought to adopt profound attitudes, which could be called *metaphysics-in-action*.

ANTONIN ARTAUD, from "Metaphysics and the Mise en Scène,"
The Theater and Its Double, 1938

But by an altogether Oriental means of expression, this objective and concrete language of the theater can fascinate and ensnare the organs. It flows into the sensibility. Abandoning Occidental usages of speech, it turns words into incantations. It extends the voice. It utilizes the vibrations and qualities of the voice. It wildly tramples rhythms underfoot. It pile-drives sounds. It seeks to exalt, to benumb, to charm, to arrest the sensibility. It liberates a new lyricism of gesture which, by its precipitation or its amplitude in the air, ends by surpassing the lyricism of words. It ultimately breaks away from the intellectual subjugation of the language, by conveying the sense of a new and deeper intellectuality which hides itself beneath the gestures and signs, raised to the dignity of particular exorcisms.

ANTONIN ARTAUD, from "The Theater of Cruelty (First Manifesto),"
The Theater and Its Double, 1938

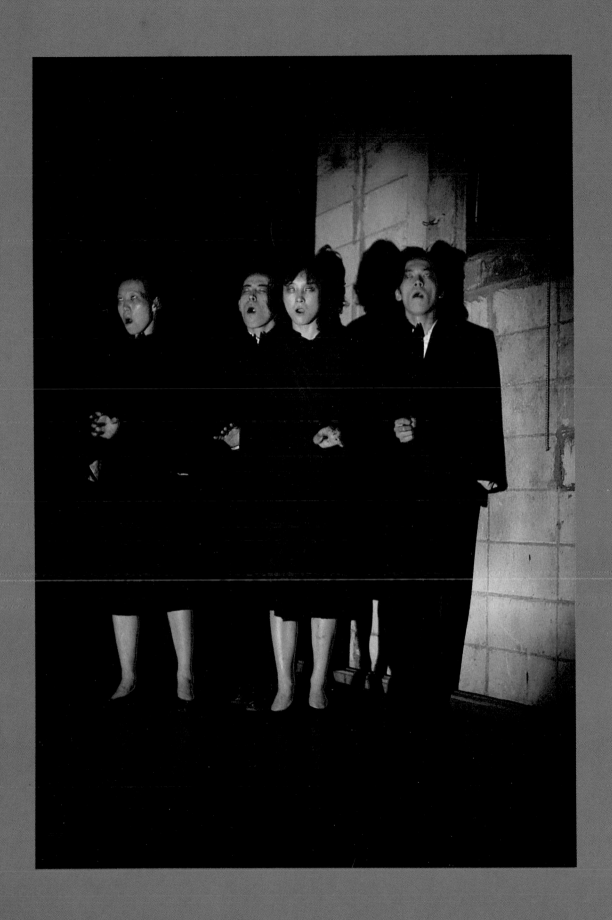

MIN TANAKA
WITH MAI JUKU
Dance: Homage to Kandinsky

The distance between image and dance

When I think of dance, the image of a pre-historic painting comes to mind. I see it traced in the deepest and darkest place in a cave, as if it hid its existence using representations other than language. I conceive it neither to live within this painting nor to experience it.

Standing in the cave

In that part of the cave which could never be made even because of the projections, the splits and outbreak in the rock, a succession of rich and eloquent images, always changing, pass my eye.

Standing in the cave, I identify myself with the painter

The painting would be drawn from intimate memories closely connected with everyday life. It would bloom on the wall with a vibrant and arresting reality, not as a simple copy of the world of the painter. This is the realisation of images issuing from the realm of the senses, and directly attached to them.

Standing in the cave, backing away from the painting

Through the painter's back, I am face to face with a wild animal. I sense the distance between myself hunting the wild animal and me that watches myself hunting the wild animal. I catch myself seeing something and hearing something. When the form appears, I realise for the first time this relation and I respond. I move from seeing to watching, and from hearing to listening.

Leave the cave.

USHIO AMAGATSU, Sankai Juku, 1982, Tokyo,
from program for *Jomon Sho*,
Sadler's Wells, London, April 1983

SANKAI JUKU
Dance: Homage to Pre-History

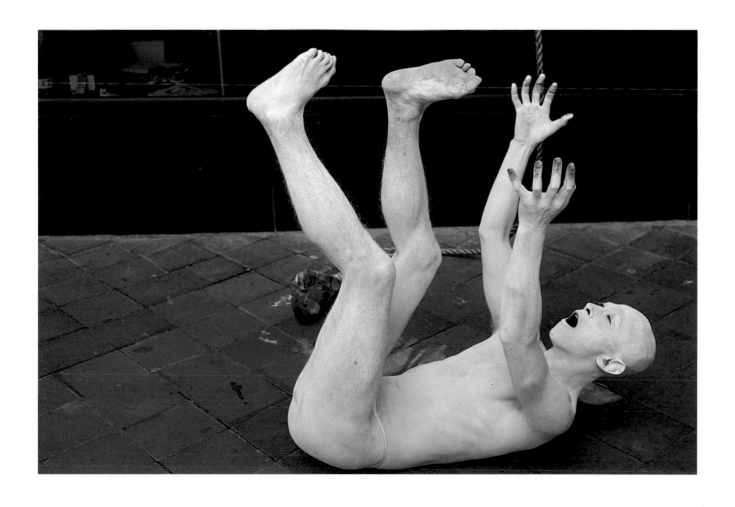

Butoh belongs both to life and death. It is a realisation of the distance between a human being and the unknown. It also represents man's struggle to overcome the distance between himself and the material world. Butoh dancers' bodies are like a cup filled to overflowing, one which cannot take one more drop of liquid—the body enters a state of perfect balance.

USHIO AMAGATSU, Sankai Juku,
from program for *Kinkan Shonen*, *The Cumquat Seed*,
Sadler's Wells, London, October 1982

We shake hands with the dead, who send us encouragement from beyond our body; this is the unlimited power of Butoh. . . . Something is hiding in our subconscious, collected in our unconscious body, which will appear in each detail of our expression. Here, we can rediscover time with an elasticity, sent by the dead. We can find Butoh in the same way we can touch our hidden reality. Something can be born, can appear, living and dying in a moment.

This cast-off skin is our land and home, which our body has forcibly ripped away. This cast-off skin is totally different from that other skin that our body has lost. They are divided in two. One skin is that of the body approved by society. The other skin is that which has lost its identity. So, they need to be sewn together, but this sewing together only forms a shadow.
 I admire our ancestors who took good care of the feeling in the soles of their feet.

TATSUMI HIJIKATA
(Edited from a translation by
Natsu Nakajima and Lizzie Slater)

Tadanori Yokoo, *The Great Mirror of the Dance as an Immolative Sacrifice*

This poster for a performance by Tatsumi Hijikata's group of dancers, *Ankoku Butoh-ha*, bears the title *Hangi Daitokan, The Great Mirror of the Dance as an Immolative Sacrifice*. The title is derived from a suggestion by the poet Mutsuro Takahashi. The calligraphy is by Yukio Mishima. *Hangi Daitokan* became an emblem for Tatsumi Hijikata; it carried the association of some ancient rite. The poster is composed from two separate poster plates. The first plate, applied in monochrome, is for a performance of *Rose-Colored Dance* by Hijikata in 1965, and it is entitled *A La Maison de M.Civeçawa (To the Shibusawa House)*, as the dance was dedicated to the novelist and translator of de Sade, Tatsuhiko Shibusawa. The two female nudes in the center of the poster are the work of Natsuyuki Nakanishi, the art director for *Ankoku Butoh-ha*, and are based on the painting *Gabrielle Distole and her Sister* by an unknown artist of the Fontainebleau school in the Louvre. Hijikata had insisted on the inclusion of Nakanishi's work and had initially suggested that Ikko Tanaka design the poster. Tanaka felt that the theme was more suited to Tadanori Yokoo and introduced the graphic designer to Hijikata. Yokoo remarked that he had never since come across anyone so enthusiastic about creating a single poster as were Hijikata or Juro Kara of the theater group *Jokyo Gekijo*. Yokoo designed a number of posters for *Jokyo Gekijo* and for the other great underground theater group of the time, Shuji Terayama's *Tenjosajiki*, of which Yokoo was a cofounder. The second plate, in color, was derived from parts of the poster for Hijikata's collaboration with the photographer Eikoh Hosoe, the dance-drama *Kamaitachi* (1968).   (Silkscreen poster, 1968, 28.7 x 40.6 in.)

KIKI NO BUYOU, DANCE OF CRISIS

By Yukio Mishima

A secret notice came to me that Tatsumi Hijikata would perform a heretic ritual again. I am already looking forward to the evening, and for my attendance I must prepare a black mask, pagan incense, and a cross with Christ smiling seductively.

When I met him the other day, Hijikata used the word "crisis" a number of times. He said, "Through dance we must depict the human posture in crisis, exactly as it is." He mentioned an example of such a posture in crisis and it was unusual: the back of a man urinating on the side of the street. Indeed he was right.

There is no doubt that almost every form of art has an awareness of crisis at its root. In primitive art, this crisis is manifested vividly in the feeling of awe toward nature; or conversely, in the extremely stylized ritual for taming nature through magic. In the arts of later periods, however, a "crisis" is called for consciously. This is also true in classical ballet. Those unnatural dance shoes, restraining the toes, seem to make human beings lose balance; they impose a sense of crisis, since the dancer is barely and perilously standing. Given this sense of crisis, the exquisite beauty of the techniques of classical ballet and of the variety of positions of balance is made possible. Yet, without the prerequisite of the "crisis of the points of dance shoes," both classical order and the beauty of balance would probably appear lifeless and cold.

Avant-garde dance does not use those dance shoes. It is clear from this that its purpose is the opposite of that of classical ballet. If the requirement of the latter is to realize "the balance at the verge of crisis," that of the former is to express the crisis itself. So avant-garde dance needs no artificial prerequisite for crisis like dance shoes. The very crisis and uncertainty of human existence must be manifested as it is through the genuine expression of the human body with little or no artificial prerequisite. It is inevitable, due to the requirement for actuality in dance, that seemingly symbolic and abstruse forms arise. Nothing (including our words) is more adorned with our practical and customary intentions than the human body. Unlike classical ballet, which takes advantage of such intentions to show the audience a false but beautiful dream, avant-garde dance must abandon such concepts from the start in order to let actuality emerge. What seems to be abstruse is but the dissonance of the act of scraping off old paint. . . . Their performance is simple, plain and very understandable.

(Translated by Kazue Kobata)

KAZEDARUMA

By Tatsumi Hijikata

In Akita, in the Tohoku region of northeastern Japan, there is a phenomenon known as *kazedaruma*, or wind *daruma* (daruma, the Japanese traditional legless doll). Great winds come raging—sometimes mixed with snow—and terrifying gusts blow and lash about, whipping the footpaths between the rice fields. Buffeted by the wind, men would appear before our door like tumblers in the wind. When these "wind darumas" would step into our sitting room, their movements, if nothing else, were like a dance. Please allow me to present my wind daruma story in that light.

At first, I was thinking of addressing "The Collection of a Weakened Body," but somehow, Tokyo people are now very busy talking of things like "Health Management" and the "Utopia of Total Health," and scurrying about on the streets. I, however, prefer to use the principle of "weakness" as a gauge, and I try to measure men based on whether or not they are overly pliable and their lives too easy. I was wondering if there was anything I'd forgotten to say about "weakness." By chance, I asked my friend Sado Ito, who lives in Kamakura, if he knew of any useful sources. He told me about a bookstore which has a volume entitled *Nihon Reiiki (Accounts of Miracles in Japan)*, and suggested that I buy it and read it. But I told him that even if I read the book I wouldn't understand it, and I asked him to read it and to make notes for me, and he agreed to do so. I have his notes in front of me.

Long ago a monk named Kyokai wrote the *Nihon Reiiki*. He'd seen himself in his own dream. It was on the seventeenth night of the third month in the year of Enryaku (A.D. 788). In his dream, Kyokai piled up firewood for his funeral pyre and cremated his own body. His spirit stood and watched over his own body being cremated but the spirit wasn't scathed by the flames as he had expected. He broke off small twigs and brought them over to poke and stab at his own flaming body. He skewered and flipped his body back and forth to help it burn, instructing those who were there for the cremation to do likewise. Gradually, the bones and joints of his limbs and his skull were all burned and fell to pieces. At that point, Kyokai's spirit made, first, a sound, and then a scream. The man next to him, however, didn't seem to hear. So Kyokai leaned over and struggled to impart his last words into the man's ear, but the man seemed to hear nothing and didn't reply.

"Ahh, my screams can't be heard because a dead man's spirit has no voice," Kyokai concluded, and recorded his thoughts.

But wait a minute; isn't that a little odd? This sentence Kyokai wrote is not something he said while he was watching the dream; it was what he recorded after he awakened. He couldn't have written it down with such ease. My "wind darumas," blown by the wind, came walking down the rice paddy path, all the while thinking the same thoughts as were recorded by a monk at his own cremation.

One was a funeral pyre, but the "wind darumas" were having

their own funeral of the wind. They're both becoming merged and muddled together. The wind darumas' spirits wanted to scream something but their voices were dissolving. They were getting larger and larger as they groped their way to the front of our house. I wonder what sort of thoughts they were having as they struggled toward our house. Now that I've combined my wind daruma story with the monk's, I sense that there's something quite ominous concealed in the spectacle of the wind darumas. The wind darumas came into the sitting room, but they didn't say much. They plopped themselves down to sit by the fire. A family member was tending the fire, but said nothing. This continued for a long time. Seeing this as a child, it was all totally inexplicable. Although I felt a vague sense of dread, it wasn't that I couldn't feel any affection toward them, and it makes me wonder just what really did happen. It was like when you receive a package first and then the letter explaining the package arrives later. Then a conversation of sorts would start:

"O-o-oo-haaa-haaaa"

("Ahh, you called out 'O-o-o' didn't you?")

"Byuuu-byuuu"

("Ahh, is it the blowing of the wind that sounded 'Byuuu-byuuu'?")

Now then, you have some understanding of these cries of "O-o-o . . . Byuuu-byuuu" and "Haa-haaaa." How dreadful was it? And those faces . . . they seemed to have returned from peering into the spirit world of the dead; they had become masks. They were neither bodies of the living nor bodies dressed up for a role in some piece of fiction or to relate a tale. They were merely lodging in a living body—bodies resurrected at "that" place! However, there were various types even among these snow darumas. There were some who came in together. They entered singing "O-o-o . . . byuuu-byuuu . . . tee-teeee . . ." Up in the north country, during the winter, we used to knock off the snow that was caught in the gaps on the bottom of our thongs in the entry hall. But even in summer we would find ourselves banging our thongs just as we had all winter. I suppose we couldn't shed ourselves of our winter habit. Anyhow, the summers were often chilly. I often shivered and shuddered even in the summer.

Sometimes only the wind came into the house; there were some wind darumas that were nothing but wind. My family was running a noodle business when I was born; the noodle shop was a sort of extension of our sitting room. This sitting room was usually empty. My brothers had all gone away to join the army, and I used to sit there all by myself; it was frightening. Even though the place was empty, every time I heard that clacking noise of the thongs, I thought it was the sound of a wind daruma coming into the house. Burning and scorching its own body, the daruma was swept by a gust along the long rice paddy paths and delivered to my house. What a fine sight!

That wind takes on a special quality in early spring, breezing over the sodden mud and soil. Once, as a child, I fell into the spring mud, and the wretched body of a child came floating up from the center. I was conscious of half-smothered screams, rising from a wooden lump somewhere around my mud-smeared stomach. Then as I went into the thick of the mud, I wondered, "Am I not some kind of bait or prey?" Those lingering thoughts from within the body were emerging. By the same token, the story illustrates the fascinating forms vested in the mud and the earth. It also encompasses the idea of the body somehow returning to the starting point at the center. Now, I was in the middle of the mud, unable to advance or retreat, when I noticed the half-closed eyes of a baby staring at me, eyes that were sleeping and yet looked wide awake. Then the head of the baby rolled closer. It's odd, isn't it? I thought it was odd! Why should a baby's head be rolling in the mud? At any rate, I was fingering this thing that looked like a baby's head, and yet I didn't feel like I was toying with it, somehow it just happened. I can't very well explain it. It did actually happen, so I am relating it as such. Even the wilting of the pumpkin flowers or the horse's cheek gowing thin can be tales of the "body." So soaking in the mud, a mouth attached itself to the sole of my foot, making slurping noises as it sucked up the mud through my sole; and a tongue of mud squeezed out between my toes. You see, the head and foot wound up inverted. The images of my wretched childhood during that spring now come fluttering back, like a wind-buffeted mud willow.

I often thought that the Japanese have come to value the soles of their feet a great deal. They walk around as if someone were going to steal their own footsteps. "Walk with the mind of a blind man," my mother often said. The idea that I was raised with my head and my soles inverted remains in me even now. But if I had presented nothing but that, it would have been mud; and if it was only mud, all of my story would be intolerable. Nevertheless, the lesson I learned from the early spring mud is that my dancing originated in a place that has no affinity with Shinto shrines and Buddhist temples. I am absolutely certain of that. I'm well aware of the fact that my present movements are built upon that particular foundation—I was born from the mud and sod.

I also had a few eccentricities. I never ate crunchy *osenbe* (rice crackers). You see, I felt that there was something unpleasant about the crunch against my teeth. I would soften them using the steam from a tea kettle and eat them after they got good and soggy. Soft, soggy, and willy-nilly—I've come to rely very much on such a physical state. It's a strange habit of mine to put myself in helpless situations. Back in the Tohoku area, they called me "a frail little imp." "What a frail little imp this one is," they'd say. Frail though I was, there was nothing around me that showed any distinctive form or shape. So you see, ultimately it comes to things like sod, mud willows, and soggy *osenbe*.

The time of these events, if I recall correctly, was the eighth year of Showa (1933). It seems that in the year I was born, the newspaper carried stories of the explosion of the Manchurian Railroad, the death of Zhang Zuo-lin, and the fact that someone named Hitomi Kinue got something or another at the Olympics. I checked on this and it really is true. It was a time when the atmosphere in Asia was gradually becoming clouded and foreboding. I was forced to eat cinders in the corner of a dirt floor.

This was to prevent worms. In the old days, when a child had worms, they were force-fed cinders rather indiscriminately. The woman who made me swallow the stuff came in from the fields and had a body that seemed to be half made of smoke. Sitting in a corner of the dirt floor, she ate pieces of cucumbers from the field. We also had soot—the soot from our kettle. I wore a kimono tied with a belt the color of that soot, and I never wore things like underpants until I went to elementary school. My heart was always racing like a dog's; "thump, thump, thump," it would pound. I suppose that was how I became such an unsettled little imp. In my boredom, I was possessed by the thought that if I didn't break the world apart, and I left it alone as it were, somehow disaster would strike. So I paced around, around, and around inside that dim house of the noodle shop. Hail would fall and it would make no difference to me.

Early spring was the busy season on the farm. Everyone went out to work in the fields. There was no one in the neighboring houses. Children three or four years old were tied to large pillars in every home. I would sneak over to take a peek at those little kids. They made strange movements; one fed food to his own hand—what an odd thing to do! Of course he was not old enough to be conscious of his self. At any rate, I was engrossed in watching this when the child's mother returned, and said, "What is it? You like kids? Please, don't come back tomorrow!" This made me feel somewhat uneasy. It was all because I went back to peek at them too often. The child was treating his hand as if it weren't a part of himself. It was as if it wasn't his own hand. He probably felt that he was someone else. From time to time, he would try to twist off his ears and all sorts of other things. Although this is a really absurd story, in it are the original movements that greatly influenced me later on in my dance. What I learned from a child's body has, to a large degree, influenced my own body.

Then when I grew older, it was the carpenter who made an impression. An expert carpenter is more accurate than the weather report. Rather than predicting the weather, he "feels" the weather. Every day he studies the humidity and the like in his wood shavings. When I used to watch my father the carpenter, I thought of him as a weather station. After strenuous work, my father would take a break and rest his hands on the table. At a casual glance, they looked like hooks or carpenter tools. Those hands—they were part of his body and yet not a part of his body! The hands of that carpenter are somehow linked to the act of that child who tried to feed his own hands. Later I'll resolve that in my dance. The substance of dance technique isn't very interesting even if I ramble on about it. I was totally enthusiastic about this concept and after some research, found this in a book:

One child attempted to feed his toes; another tried to show the calf of his leg the scenery outside the room; there is yet another who tried to move the garden rocks in order to show them new scenery.

Ahh, see, isn't this just like what I saw? I once actually took the water dipper from the kitchen sink and secretly put it out in the field. I put it out there, thinking that it was a pity for

teaching a stone to talk.

125

it to be in the cupboard, where the sun never shines. So I tried to show the outside scenery in the field to the water dipper. Taking into your own body the idea that your wrist is not your own—there's an important secret hidden in this concept. The basis of dance is concealed there.

Now then, I can also imagine it this way . . . let's see: "I am an empty box, too!" Then from the inside comes a reply, "We're just like a couple of mortuary urns, aren't we?" So you see, by and by communication emerges. I may also be a wicker trunk, crushed into the shape of bellows, with all of my insides scattered all over the street, and having a great time of it. Finally, I see a horse standing there, and I feel an urge to cut it with a saw . . . or rather, I'm going to cut up the river. It would be good if the river's frozen, so yes, cut up the river and bring it back. Thereupon my body rapidly begins to expand and gets wider and wider. It's the sky . . . yes, indeed! I could have imagined that to be a plate, then I could have cut it in half with one blow. But then, that single plate is also a body-plate, isn't it? If I cut that in half, it's likely to cause a riot. The expansion of the body, which doesn't have anything to do with these fantasies, is spreading more and more quickly.

Now, when early spring came, the water from the melting snow would rush into the river, creating a whirlpool. I would jump into that vortex and be seized by the root of a willow tree. The grown-ups would come searching for me yelling, "What happened? Is he dead?" Soon I would be rescued from the whirlpool. There and then I would be born again; I was born! Over and over, I was born and transformed. It was no longer enough to be born only from the womb. I was born many times over; I used to carry out this experiment regardless of where I was. In the old days, everybody filled jugs with water. I'd take my sickle and cut at the water in the jug. "Separate into two," I'd command. This act somehow seemed to make time stand still. I wonder if this experience is yet another blood relative to my dance. It can't be acquired through training; it's something that your body teaches itself. I always used to say about my dancing, "I'm a dancer neither of experience nor of mastery through practice." When you encounter such experiences, things will emerge from your body naturally. I've often said in the past that we don't have time to "express" and "represent."

Actually, my story is not always so hectic. This clever little imp, who was always conscious of his gullible insides, would at times pretend to be an idiot with his mouth hanging open. The grown-ups used to catch my eye when I stared out into the streets. There was one who walked by, trying to catch up with his own body, then there was a man breathing hard as he trudged along, chased by his own body. I watched these things with a frenetic excitement. But it often rained, and at those times I sat on the veranda and watched the rain fall into the cabbage patch. The veranda was important to me. The rain seemed to be without beginning or end; as it fell, time and space became mixed and entwined, until no distinction remained between the two. And then, like rotting cabbage, I, too, seemed to deteriorate from the center. Japanese dance often refers to this "center," or *ma*. *Ma* in dance also rots; they call it "spatial decay," or *makusare*. When this happens, it is nothing less than disaster. It'll drive people to run and hide in their closets. This is probably hard to imagine when you're watching from the outside; but I've been grappling desperately with this problem.

So various things went on like this . . . events that occurred and those that didn't . . . they were all there. When I rouse myself to think about them, I get carried away by the image of myself at grammar school, pattering down the long corridors like a sperm. I fluttered unsteadily along, a sperm pushed forth by the rhythm. Though I wouldn't let anyone see, tears pour down in spite of myself when I recall my youth.

Let me tell you a story about my mother—well, it's not actually about my mother as such. Anyhow, when the snow came down making a sort of pitter-patter sound, my mother would add the pitter-patter of little feet by bearing children. There were eleven of us, and I was the youngest. She was back in the kitchen washing dishes the day after she bore me. Since there were eleven of us I had plenty of older brothers and sisters. All my brothers went into the army. Before they left, my father let them drink sake from special sake cups and sent them off saying, "Do a good job and come back!" After the sake, all their faces turned bright red . . . serious young men, my brothers were! But when they came back, they were ashes in mortuary urns. They turned bright red when they left, and turned to ashes when they came back.

Those times and those shapes, having vanished, manifest themselves through their disintegration; the shapes have become distinct and vivid. Back then, I didn't think about such things, but now that the years have passed, they are coming back to haunt my mind. I wonder if my mother thought about them in the same way. As a child, I didn't like going to school, and neither of my parents insisted, unlike today's families. Anyway, I wasn't too keen on going, but I often couldn't decide whether I should or not. I'd vacillate between wanting to stay home and wanting to go, and finally I'd end up sitting on the side of the road, with my knees apart. As I sat there, the open spaces in my knees would grow wider and wider, and my thoughts would wander. "Ahh, I suppose it's all right not to go . . . should I do this . . . or should I do that just like my knees, one to the other . . . so I disjointed my knees and sat by the roadside. The open spaces in my disjointed knees extended wider and wider from the confines I imagined in my head. In this great expanse, my mind would wander, "Ahh, I guess it's okay not to go . . . should I do this . . . or should I do that . . . it would be nice for my body to be all disjointed . . . ."

That's how I spent my youth, and at any rate, I guess I've painted the gestures and deportment of the lady next door, my parents, and my family like those of a thieving cat. Because there was nothing else with which to amuse myself, I have hidden all these things inside me. The movements of the dog next door and such are like so many broken boats, drifting inside me in bits and pieces. From time to time, however, these boats gather, speak, and consume the darkness—the most valuable food source inside my body. And sometimes their body and hand gestures that collect within me get attached to my hands, and surface.

When I want to hold an object, one hand reaches out, but the other hand tries to hold it back . . . one hand chases the other. My hands grow so weak I can't reach the object. In time, one hand reaches out and won't come back; sometimes it disappears while it reaches and other times it vanishes while it's over the object. If you watch and listen carefully, you'll realize that I'm not lying or rambling because I'm hard-pressed for something to say. I've noticed these occurrences in animals, too. I've even noticed them in the neighborhood dogs.

Let's now talk about something that is easy to understand: raising silkworms. Over there a man's raising silkworms. The noise of the silkworms chewing on mulberry leaves is endless—"*jyari-jyari-jyari*"—it goes on and on. If the man takes a nap while this goes on he'll gnash his teeth "*giri-giri-giri*." As the silkworms chew on, the sound of their chewing becomes synchronized with the sound of the gnashing of teeth. What you hear is the harmony of the two sounds. When the man awakens, his cotton robe has turned completely green. He gets up and steps into the room where the silkworms are chewing away, and he keeps on gnashing his teeth. All the elements are linked to each other. If matters always work as they do here, I wonder if dance training is really necessary. Well, it's something to think about.

To make gestures of the dead, to die again, to make the dead reenact once more their deaths in their entirety—these are what I want to experience within me. A person who has died once can die over and over again within me. Moreover, I've often said although I'm not acquainted with Death, Death knows me. I have an older sister living inside me. When I'm engrossed in dance creation, she tears at the darkness within me and consumes more than she needs to. If she stands, I sit down without thinking about it; if I stumble, she too stumbles. There's an undeniable connection. She once said to me, "Although you perform upon reaching the ecstasy of dance and expression, isn't it true that your ability to express depends upon the inexpressible?" and having thus spoken, she vanished. So you see, she's my teacher; the dead are my teachers. We should take good care of our deceased. Sooner or later, we too will be summoned. That's why we've got to learn these dreadful lessons while we're still alive; that's how we can keep our wits about us when the time comes. We've got to bring the dead close to us and lead our lives with them. There's nothing but brightness now. But I wonder if this brightness didn't arrive on the back of the darkness within us. That little imp threw his weight about and ate recklessly in the darkness; so the darkness escaped from the night. There is no darkness in the night now. In the old days, the darkness was so crystal clear.

Let's move the current of the wind to the fields. We used to have something called an *izume*. They were woven straw baskets usually used to keep the rice warm. When the grown-ups went to work in the field, they'd take the small children along in the baskets. Four or five kids would be placed haphazardly in the middle of the field in one of these. Inevitably one of them in the middle of the heap would have an "accident" and get a diaper rash all over his lower torso. Not able to move because he's crammed in with other kids and a bunch of other things and unable to do anything to ease his distress, the kid cries. But no matter how hard he cries, his mother ignores him. It's hard for the grown-ups too. They're working overtime and the work is back-breaking hard labor. They can't let up. Meanwhile, the kid's screaming as loud as ever but his cries are getting drowned by the roar of the wind in the damp and wide-open air. His cries are no longer being heard by the grown-ups. His throat is getting swollen, his eyes dim. Finally, he passes out. While he drifts in and out of consciousness, he realizes that crying is useless. His eyes refuse to surface from the pool of tears; his eyes and tears dry up on his cheeks. The child is torn and consumed by all of this. He is torn and consumed by the darkness. I wonder what the child is thinking. I know that a child would not really think this way, but I can imagine him thinking, "The sky is damned idiotic; this is a damned cemetery!" It's fine to call the sky nasty names, but from the very beginning the child was placed in the middle of the contraption so that his cries wouldn't be heard. He has to learn to amuse himself with his own body as a toy and to learn to tear and consume the darkness. Then when night falls, the child is taken out of his place of torment. But because his feet had been so scrunched up he can't straighten them out, let alone stand. The grown-ups, at that point, gather in a circle to watch, with faint smiles on their lips. The child's face, however, is solemn. He doesn't want to see his parents' faces any longer. Where was I walking to when I was left jammed in there? No matter how much I talk about this, I can't seem to say enough.

I don't think this is just a story about dance. But even with our ways of expressing ourselves, is it really possible to arrive at one's true destination? These kinds of questions are inherent in the child's crammed feet . . . . Words fail me here. Maybe "bow-legged" is a better way to describe it. Regarding this point, the foreigners have a straightforward way of looking at these things. They say that one should dance on straight, stiffened feet. The children and also the working grown-ups have gone back and forth from life to death too often, so often that their feet have become two sticks bent at the joints. They make hollow tapping noises as they walk. There are also those who are one-legged. The children were carried in baskets on their way home.

Well, you really should try living with the dead. It'll put you in touch with a hidden flavor and that flavor will add zest to your life and tastes. Once you sprinkle it on, it'll be truly delectable! "Ahh . . . nurse, is it time?" How I long to see it! Now if you watch the dance tomorrow with this frame of mind, you'll probably understand it.

From a speech given on the eve of the Butoh Festival '85
Tokyo, February 9, 1985
(Translated by Nippon Services Corporation, New York)

AFTERWORD
By Haven O'More

Butoh is created in the mother's womb as life is, and its energy and mechanism should be the same. The world of Butoh must be that of the mother's womb.

KAZUO OHNO

Butoh deals directly with the mind through its art of dance.

But *what* does this mean?

It means Butoh makes its striking impression by skillful interpositions of silence and sound, nakedness and various levels of dress, stillness and motion.

To say Butoh deals directly with the mind includes two levels of understanding. First, we understand that mind involves functions of consciousness or awareness *and* so-called subconsciousness or non-aware functions not immediately evident to waking-state consciousness; further, mind includes tie-ins to higher levels of integration which, in their collectivity, function as intelligence or light-giving procedures for both thought and action. Second, we understand that the vastly greater part of mind (if we may even speak of mind as having a "part") remains hidden and largely unknown.

That art which reveals to us more of the hidden and unknown gives us more awareness. Awareness, in turn, gives us superior control: we are less the victims of chance and impulse—our own and the apparent randomness that can come about through the actions of other persons and circumstances. In the beginning the artist does not always necessarily set out to gain deeper control over consciousness by increasing understanding, but great art does provide this. And we feel that art to be the very greatest which goes furthest in opening up the hidden and unknown territory of the mind into the *now* known.

In the course of a two-hour performance, Hijikata started as a thirty-nine year old, and gradually he became younger and younger. He became thirty-five, then he was twenty-five, eighteen, twelve, and I remember thinking there must be a secret. This must be the secret of dance.

YOKO ASHIKAWA

There are few aspects of any art where the creative unconscious or subconscious, with extremes of force and possibility, is displayed in an objective manner. As examples, poetry and music provide displays through rhythms and structures. Dance interacts with time, mo-tion, and the human body developing spontaneous structures.

The concept of the creative subconscious being on view before an audience becomes even more powerful when held up against psychoanalysis as advanced by Freud and company—psychoanalysts who have been trying for the better part of a century now to "explain" and "treat" the subconscious.

Explain it, treat it? Yes, but how to explain, how to treat? Explaining and treating frequently probes the negative and destructive associations of the subconscious. It is valuable to make the dark, negative, destructive associations of the subconscious more apparent. That the subconscious has a state of being is not a new discovery, certainly not by psychoanalysis. Freud's writings, for example, are full of references to earlier literature, and Freud was much moved by poetry. He especially studied the Bible, to mention only one supreme case. Freud became aware that the text of the Bible leads all the way through the subconscious (hell) to transcendence (heaven). As the biblical text shows, no one has ever risen to heaven except through sacrifice and death, followed by the awakening that takes place in hell. The New Testament testifies to the major event in the Bible: Christ after his crucifixion (sacrifice) and death descended into hell for three days. Afterwards he appeared back among men as witness to the overcoming of death before ascending to heaven.

When I trained to dance like a baby, the one thing that was most important to me was to explore and find the light.

YOKO ASHIKAWA

Doesn't the subconscious have other forces; is the destructive its dominant force? Surely not. Butoh demonstrates that the subconscious is enormously more creative than destructive.

Butoh brings the subconscious before our very eyes, allowing us to see it and hear it and smell it in creative interaction. But what is the purpose of this? Is Butoh not ugly at times? Is Butoh not messy? Is Butoh not, even, frequently disgusting to a properly organized, clean, wholesome mind? We must answer yes to these questions. However, before we look at this further, we must say what Butoh is not.

Butoh is not religious, nor is it non-religious. Butoh is not humanistic. Butoh professes nothing: no personality cult, no religion, no political this-or-that, no *ism*. Butoh does not profess. Butoh insists over and over: let us get at the truth. *Nothing else, nothing but the truth . . .* Mind, to be dis-ease free, demands truth. We begin to contemplate Butoh from this point.

The Butoh costume is like throwing the cosmos onto one's shoulders. And for Butoh, while the costume covers the body, it is the body that is the costume of the soul.

KAZUO OHNO

Now, what about the properly organized, clean, wholesome, completely "rational" believing-completely-in-this-or-that-mind? Such a mind is poisoned. Such a mind breeds pestilence. In fact, this mind gives life over to pestilence. Such a mind sets up false gods; it makes merciless war on all creation.

Butoh is hard on such a mind. Butoh is almost as hard on such a mind as the man or woman having such a mind is hard on him or herself. Civilization from its earliest times until now—especially now, in these times shows nothing is harder on everyone, living and dead, than a properly organized, clean, wholesome, believing-completely-in-this-or-that-ism mind. Such a mind can be summed up in one word as a chthonic mind, one driven by the forces of the infernal deities. In short, a thoroughly modern mind!

Butoh opposes diseased mind. Butoh would have mind holy—whole and healthy. Butoh demonstrates for us, as William Blake has said, "For everything that lives is holy, life delights in life." Butoh shows and reminds us: "life delights in life." This, more precisely, is to say that Butoh's art endeavors *to help us find out our own mind and creatively release its contents*. All true art reaches out toward this. Great art achieves it.

Butoh enters the deepest darkness. Light pierces the opaque. Dealing directly before us with the body, Butoh strips the body to its essence. Butoh takes the body as it finds it. Butoh begins working with the body. Butoh wishes to teach the body but it also submits itself to learning from the body. What would the body be taught and what would it teach? Would it not wish to be taught and to teach about light? Would it not be taught that to really understand light it must enter into darkness: that the body must re-enter the womb. From the womb being *aware* that it is in the womb, the body can begin its integration process. It can begin to know.

Butoh enacts the womb and its contents and its struggles before our eyes. We are there in the womb; we are struggling in the womb; we are wishing to be born from the womb; we are fighting for light; we *want*, we must have experience; we demand knowledge: at birth *with each breath we demand knowledge*! Butoh takes us into this world of life and death enacted both within us and before us.

Butoh (dance) is not the dance of the epoch. It is said that Butoh was the manifestation of a desire for metamorphosis. But I don't think so. Butoh engaged itself in a combat with a painted body, but the body remained raw. Tatsumi Hijikata longed for nothing.

MIN TANAKA

Butoh becomes the search into the mind. For the mind to be the creative mind it must return, over and over, to its origins. We must long for nothing but to return to the endlessness of the cosmos, to be reborn. Min Tanaka tells us "Tatsumi Hijikata longed for nothing." He longed for nothing, that is, except to be born over and over. As he himself says, "I was born and transformed. It was no longer enough to be born only from the womb."

When Hijikata speaks of "dying again" and making "gestures of the dead," he is speaking of memory and the real necessity of going into memory to make contact with the dead both within us and without. This means one must connect with one's own dead: with the generations of the dead one is descended from, through many levels, to be in this life. It also means appropriating the dead, their deaths, their lives, within one's own life in order to become more fully alive with each breath, with each instant more full both to oneself and to other human beings. This means becoming more aware-conscious. And to become more aware-conscious means to become more creative, more helpful, more loving.

What was mystery becomes creative and transforming force. Artist and audience reach for the light together: they struggle together, they suffer together, they love together, they grow together, they find knowledge together, they celebrate together.

Let us, now, celebrate this new form of dance. Let us not condemn ourselves, let us celebrate ourselves! Let us celebrate Butoh together!

We shake hands with the dead, who send us encouragement from beyond our body; this is the unlimited power of Butoh.

TATSUMI HIJIKATA

TATSUMI HIJIKATA
IN MEMORIAM
1928–1986

To make gestures of the dead, to die again, to make the dead reenact once more their deaths in their entirety—these are what I want to experience within me. A person who has died once can die over and over again within me. Moreover, I've often said although I'm not acquainted with Death, Death knows me.

TATSUMI HIJIKATA 1985